REACHING
the
Reluctant Writer

FAST, FUN INFORMATIONAL WRITING IDEAS

Mike Artell

Maupin House

Reaching the Reluctant Writer
FAST, FUN INFORMATIONAL WRITING IDEAS

Original Illustrations................ Mike Artell
Cover Design & Page Layout .... Hank McAfee
Editor....................................... Erica Dix

Library of Congress Cataloging-in-Publication Data

Artell, Mike.
  Reaching the reluctant writer : fast, fun, informational writing ideas /
Mike Artell.
     p. cm.
  Includes bibliographical references.
  ISBN 0-929895-79-7 (pbk.)
  1. English language--Composition and exercises--Study and teaching (Middle
school)--Activity programs. 2. Language arts (Middle school)--Activity
programs. I. Title.
  LB1631.A683 2005
  808'.042'0712--dc22
                              2005005477

To schedule a school visit or workshop with Mike Artell, visit:
www.mikeartell.com or write to: P.O. Box 3997, Covington, LA 70434

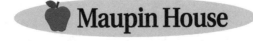

Maupin House Publishing, Inc.
PO Box 90148 • Gainesville, FL 32607
1-800-524-0634 • 352-373-5588 • 352-373-5546 (fax)

www.maupinhouse.com • email: info@maupinhouse.com

Publishing Professional Resources that Improve Classroom Performance

Dedication

This book is dedicated to all those wonderful kids who are naturally funny.

Table of Contents

Introduction

Most writing instruction for upper elementary and middle school students focuses on the techniques and conventions common to fictional texts. When students study elements of fiction like plot, dialogue, characterization, and voice, they practice a form of writing that aims to inspire or entertain readers. But what about the writing we see on a daily basis, such as ad copy, websites, product information, and how-to texts that specifically attempt to inform or persuade readers? What writing techniques or conventions should students learn to help them become better writers and readers of such "real world" texts?

Although it is necessary and important for young people to practice writing fiction, the fact is that most students will not grow up to be novelists or playwrights. Most of them, however, will find themselves regularly writing emails, reports, evaluations, memos, and instructions. This kind of writing is known as "non-fiction" or "informational" writing. Like poetry and prose, effective informational writing can entertain and inspire, as well as persuade, motivate, and inform readers. Thus, the purpose of this book is to develop your students' ability to write clear, functional, and creative non-fiction texts.

Developing and encouraging the reluctant writer

Though all students will benefit from the exercises outlined in this book, the larger purpose of *Reaching the Reluctant Writer* is to engage those students who are typically bored with or overwhelmed by traditional writing instruction. We're all "reluctant writers" when the subject we are writing about fails to interest us or deals with topics about which we have no opinion, and students are no different. Furthermore, I believe that many young people find the very act of writing to be an intimidating task. If the sheer thought of composing and editing detailed stories, reports, and essays isn't daunting enough for students, the idea of having a teacher then read and evaluate their writing for errors and inconsistencies can be downright panic-inducing. As a result, some students procrastinate, tune out, and perform poorly on writing assignments; behavior which can set the course for subsequent writing experiences.

Reaching the Reluctant Writer provides young writers with some much needed encouragement through a series of short, light writing exercises that stimulate creativity and contain "real world" relevance. As students cultivate confidence in their ability to write short pieces well, they will be better equipped to craft works of greater depth and sophistication. In addition, the 43 exercises in this book:

- allow teachers to focus their writing instruction on the development of specific writing craft skills,
- lend themselves to humor and cleverness by making writing delightful and fun,
- tie in well with other forms of communication, such as drawing, drama, and music,
- give students an opportunity to write something with a beginning, a middle, and an end, and
- maintain students' interest by allowing them to write short, creative, and practical everyday texts.

What is "thinking funny"?

You'll notice that the phrase "think funny" appears often in this book and that humor plays an integral role in many of the writing exercises. I find humor to be a greatly underused educational tool that requires and elicits many different talents and skills from students. If students can use humor to express viewpoints, reinforce opinions, or simply make classmates laugh, they will be much more likely to find the creative courage to put their thoughts down on paper.

Moreover, many reluctant writers in particular thrive in an instructional environment that encourages inventive, original thinking. Humor gives these students an opportunity to exercise the "funny side" of their brains and approach writing tasks from a unique and inspired perspective.

Why are drawings important to informational writing?

Although this is a writing book, each exercise includes a visual component that challenges students to create their own artwork and design functional layouts for the various informational texts they compose. This artistic element develops the visual literacy skills that will help students incorporate another sense—sight—into their written communication. In our increasingly image-based world, young people are learning to read images as another language. Video games, fast-paced television advertisements, and billboards are just a few examples of visual texts that inform, persuade, and motivate readers through a combination of images and text. It is both relevant and necessary that students understand the communicative potential of visual information and practice integrating images into their own writing.

Working with images will also help young writers clarify and reinforce the thoughts and ideas they are trying to get across on paper. For example, in the "Classified Advertisement" exercise on page 17, students must draw a picture of an item they are selling to include with ad copy they have previously written. Here, the image and text work together to ensure the accuracy, comprehensiveness, and clarity of the overall ad, as students' drawings may reveal an important feature of the item that they neglected to emphasize in their written ad. The ability to think visually and textually bolsters student creativity and helps young writers express themselves more effectively in today's visual culture.

A note about format

As you flip through this book, you'll find a specific format that allows you to administer each writing exercise during class in six easy steps. You begin with the "Prepare" section, which details any materials or research you need to gather before class. Then, the "Discuss" section provides you with a series of topics and question prompts to generate an engaging and dynamic class discussion about a particular everyday text. Also, the "Writing skill" section specifies the individual writing craft skills that each exercise develops, allowing you to customize this book to serve your own instructional needs and goals.

Next, the "Write" and "Draw" sections challenge students to compose an informational text and create a visual element that will accompany or reinforce their writing. Last, a set of "Assessment" questions tailored to each exercise will help you evaluate the strengths and weaknesses of a student's participation and performance.

Some exercises feature an additional "Invite a speaker" section that suggests professionals who may be able to provide some added insight into the informational text or topic under discussion. The writing exercises are presented in alphabetical order; they can be done in sequence, or you may wish to select exercises that highlight specific writing craft skills your students need help mastering. Ultimately, you know your students best, so use this book in a way that works best for them.

About the Author

PREPARE

Prepare: Advise the school's media specialist that your students will be studying "About the Author" copy on the dust jackets of several books, preferably autobiographies. Ask the media specialist to choose some developmentally appropriate books that include interesting information about the author on the dust jackets.

DISCUSS

Discuss: After students have studied the "About the Author" text, ask them to identify the different types of information included, such as the authors' birthplace, profession, awards they have received, etc. Also, point out that "About the Author" text is generally written in the third person, even if the book is an autobiography. Then, tell students to count the number of sentences that appear in the dust jacket information, and explain that "About the Author" text merely highlights and summarizes interesting author facts and details.

Next, compare photos of authors from several book jackets and discuss the similarities and differences between them. Do the photos differ if the author is known as a serious or silly person? In addition, ask students to describe the different fonts used in the "About the Author" texts. Do "serious" autobiographies feature non-serif fonts, or do "silly" books include fonts that are looser or more embellished?

Writing skill: Use supporting details
As students write about the person they know best (themselves), they'll reveal hobbies, interests, backgrounds, and other interesting character traits that help readers "flesh out" or visualize the writer. The ability to develop characters through the use of supporting details is important when writing biographies or fiction. Once students learn to write about their own character traits, they can apply that skill to writing about other people or characters.

About the Author

WRITE

Write: Students will compose "About the Author" text that would appear on the dust jacket of their autobiographies. Dust jacket information should be one paragraph in length and written in the third person. Encourage students to include supporting details about themselves that are specific and descriptive. For instance, the statement, "John likes to play guitar. John has one sister and a dog," could be embellished with descriptive adjectives to read, "John's favorite hobby is playing his Fender™ electric guitar. He has an older sister who is always telling him what to do and a seven-year-old black lab named Wrecks."

DRAW

Draw: Students will draw self-portraits to include with their dust jacket information. Resist the temptation to let students use photos of themselves since hand-drawn portraits more accurately reveal a student's self-perception. Students can create simple black-and-white line drawings or full-color portraits.

ASSESSMENT

✓ Did the student participate in the class discussion?

✓ Did the student write "About the Author" text in the third person?

✓ Did the student's "About the Author" text provide some interesting or amusing information about the student rather than just "dry" facts?

✓ Did the student use supporting details to flesh out the autobiographical information?

✓ Did the student make a good faith effort to draw a self-portrait?

Advice Column

PREPARE

Prepare: Cut out advice columns, such as "Dear Abby," from your local newspaper or from magazines for young people. If possible, try to collect advice columns that are presented in a letter format. Then, bring the samples you gathered to class and pass them around to your students.

DISCUSS

Discuss: Read one or two of the advice columns aloud to your students and discuss the different emotions expressed by writers, like grief, anxiety, fear, angst, etc. Encourage students to share who they go to when they need advice and why they find that person helpful. Then, point out that advice columnists typically have relevant professional credentials or are popularly recognized for their commonsense guidance.

Next, note that most writers solicit advice in the form of a letter, and challenge students to name the different parts of a letter, such as the greeting, body, and closing. Also, mention that some advice columns discourage writers from submitting their names, and indicate any clever examples of how writers veil their identities (e.g., "Sincerely, Confused in Baltimore"). Finally, explain that advice columns in magazines and newspapers must fit within a specific, fixed space, which means writers seeking advice must present their problems in as few words as possible.

Writing skill: Letter-writing
This exercise allows students to practice their letter-writing skills, as students are challenged to compose letters with a greeting, a body, and a closing. In addition, students will gain a better understanding of voice as they adopt the first person point of view to express the woes of a famous folk/fairy tale character.

Advice Column

WRITE

Write: Students will pose as folk/fairy tale characters, such as Little Red Riding Hood or Goldilocks, and write a letter to Mother Goose asking for advice on how to solve a problem. Students' letters must include a greeting, body, and closing and establish the reasons for their characters' distress. Also, encourage students to be creative and "think funny" when assuming different voices and brainstorming clever monikers to "conceal" their character's identity. Here's an example:

Dear Mother Goose,

My two stepsisters make me do all the work. My stepmother hates me and says I can't go to the ball. What can I do?

Sincerely,
Lonely in the Castle

DRAW

Draw: Students can embellish their letters with borders, fonts, and spot art that reflect their character's persona or situation. For instance, Cinderella's letter could be covered in soot smudges or Goldilocks's letter might be decorated with porridge stains and strands of yellow hair.

ASSESSMENT

✓ Did the student participate in the class discussion?

✓ Did the student clearly state a problem for which the character needs help?

✓ Has the student used humor in any way in the letter?

✓ Has the student identified the character to Mother Goose in an interesting or unusually descriptive way?

✓ Did the student embellish the letter with borders, fonts, or spot art representative of the chosen folk/fairy tale character?

Back Cover Copy

Prepare: Check out several fiction and non-fiction books from your school library that feature well-written back cover copy, and bring them to class. Also, be sure to collect books that are appropriate to your students' grade and reading level.

DISCUSS

Discuss: Pass the books around and allow students to read the back covers. Then, challenge the class to identify the different kinds of information detailed in the back cover text, such as a content summary, favorable reviews for the book, brief biographical information about the author, etc. Do students find that their curiosity or interest in any of the books has been piqued since reading the back cover copy? Explain that the purpose of back cover text is to inform readers about the book and persuade them to read further.

Next, read the back cover copy for one of the fiction books you selected aloud to the class, instructing students beforehand to write down any descriptive words or phrases they recognize. Repeat this activity with a non-fiction text as well, and ask students to discuss the similarities and differences between the back cover copy in fiction and non-fiction books. For instance, do the back cover texts in fictional books feature more vivid adjectives and plot-driven summaries while the back covers of non-fiction texts emphasize the educational or instructive value of the book?

Finally, note the use of any language or writing techniques meant to intrigue the audience, like the inclusion of short excerpts or quotes from the narrative, and talk about the importance of engaging readers before they even open a book.

Writing skill: Writing to engage readers
In this exercise, students will practice summarizing familiar narratives in a way that engages and captures the interest of readers. The ability to "hook" an audience or appeal to readers is an important skill for young writers learning to combine persuasive and informative writing. Moreover, when students draft back cover copy, they get an opportunity to write in a format that is both informative and creative.

Reaching the Reluctant Writer

Back Cover Copy

WRITE

Write: Students will draft the back cover copy for a fictional book or story that they have read. You can assign students a popular folk/fairy tale with which they are all familiar, such as *Little Red Riding Hood*, or students can pick a favorite story that you approve beforehand.

Students' back cover copy must briefly summarize what the narrative is about, feature at least five descriptive words or phrases, and include three mock reviews of the story (e.g., "A critical masterpiece. The saga of *The Three Little Pigs* is a searing drama that resounds with barnyard animals of all generations"—*The Ranch Review*). Also, remind students to choose quotes or passages from the narrative to include in the back cover copy that will captivate and intrigue readers.

DRAW

Draw: Students will create book jackets that display the story title, original front cover art, and the back cover copy they have written. Provide students with construction paper, paper grocery bags, or the blank, undecorated side of wrapping paper. Students can create book jackets by covering their textbooks in the paper you provide them with.

In addition, remind students to draw inspiration from the narrative's plot or main themes when illustrating their book jackets. Encourage the use of creative design elements, like borders, attractive colors, and interesting font styles.

ASSESSMENT

✓ Did the student participate in the class discussion?

✓ Did the student's back cover copy adequately summarize the plot of the story?

✓ Did the student's back cover copy include five descriptive adjectives and three mock reviews?

✓ Did the student include intriguing quotes or passages from the book in the back cover copy to capture reader interest?

✓ Was the student able to create a book jacket that featured the story title, original cover art, and the back cover copy?

✓ Did the student experiment with different fonts, colors, and border art when illustrating the book jacket?

Brochures

PREPARE

Prepare: Research famous cities and ports of call with your students and check online travel websites to determine the airfare, hotel costs, and rental car fees for a trip to one of these locales. Also, gather some travel brochures and ask students to study the information provided, as well as the brochure's layout and design.

DISCUSS

Discuss: Encourage students to discuss which brochures they think are the most visually appealing and/or well-written, and ask them to identify the pictures featured in the brochures as romantic, exotic, adventurous, etc. Then, point out any descriptive adjectives used in the brochure's text, such as "glamorous," "mysterious," or "sun-drenched," and talk about how these words help the reader visualize the place described. After reading the text in the brochures, would students like to visit any of the locales?

Next, list the different types of information common to the brochures, like contact information, pricing, and descriptive text, on the chalkboard or overhead. Also, discuss the design and layout of the brochures, including the placement of graphics and text. Do students think the graphics relate to the text provided? Finally, challenge the class to identify what audience the writers of the brochures are targeting and whether or not travel brochures are persuasive, informative, motivational, or some combination of the three.

Invite a speaker: Invite a parent or other adult who works in advertising, public relations, or for a newspaper or printing company to speak to your class about how to create effective brochures.

Writing skill: Using descriptive adjectives
This exercise challenges students to use descriptive adjectives freely without being redundant or misleading. In creating their own travel brochures, young writers practice crafting short, punchy text that will inform, persuade, and motivate readers through the use of engaging and inviting descriptive details.

Brochures

WRITE

Write: Students will work in small groups to create travel brochures for places they have visited or would like to visit. Encourage students to use descriptive adjectives that engage and entice readers to visit the locale. In addition, travel brochures should include the following information:

- Name of location
- Description of location
- Contact information (including phone number, website address, etc.)
- Pricing
- Quotes from people who have visited this locale

Remind groups to refer to the brochures you brought to class as models.

DRAW

Draw: Students will now design a layout for their brochures using a single piece of copy paper folded into thirds as a brochure template. Instruct students to display the content they have written on the brochure panels, along with original artwork depicting different pictures of the locale. Also, advise groups to experiment with different colors, fonts, and borders when illustrating their brochures.

ASSESSMENT

✓ Did the student participate in the class discussion?

✓ Did the student contribute to the group?

✓ Did the group include descriptive adjectives that would motivate readers to visit the locale?

✓ Did the brochure include the required information?

✓ Did the group design a layout for their brochure that featured original artwork, interesting fonts, and attractive colors?

Bumper Stickers

PREPARE

Prepare: As you're driving, walking, or biking, pay attention to the bumper stickers you see on vehicles and write down any memorable bumper sticker captions. Try to collect a variety of bumper sticker statements, including funny ones, and bring them to class.

DISCUSS

Discuss: Read the bumper sticker captions aloud to your students and challenge them to explain what each caption means. Do students find the bumper sticker statements forceful, intriguing, funny, or confusing? Then, ask students to discuss which statements they liked and why. Explain that bumper sticker captions generally reflect a point of view, support a cause, or express some sentiment the driver endorses.

Next, read the bumper sticker captions aloud a second time and ask students to count how many words are used in each statement. Also, note the length of the average bumper sticker and talk about how the limited space forces the writer to craft short, succinct statements that will capture the interest of other drivers. Last, point out the use of bold colors, fonts, and capitalized text in bumper stickers, and discuss how these visual elements draw attention to the caption displayed.

Writing skill: Be concise
This activity challenges students to craft compelling yet concise statements that will attract readers. Though this style of writing is difficult, young writers will note how powerful their messages sound when expressed succinctly and should be empowered to incorporate this technique into longer texts as well.

Bumper Stickers

WRITE

Write: Groups of two to three students will compose bumper sticker captions that express a viewpoint/sentiment or support a cause. Students can create mock bumper stickers by cutting legal-sized paper lengthwise (two bumper stickers per sheet). Also, your local office supply store, educational supply store, or printing shop may have blank bumper sticker paper already cut to size with a sticky backing.

Students can include some spot art on their bumper stickers, but the focus should be on the text, not the art. In addition, bumper stickers must make a clear, strong statement or ask a provocative question in ten words or less. Here's an example:

We don't need your trash!
Please dispose of litter properly.

A statement like "Have a nice day" is not powerful enough for a bumper sticker, which should carry the visual impact of a full-size poster.

DRAW

Draw: Groups will choose font styles and colors that draw attention to their bumper sticker captions. Remind students that text is the "artwork" in this exercise, so they should put as much thought into the layout and design of the bumper sticker as they would a typical drawing or illustration. Also, encourage the use of bold fonts and capitalized letters, as well as vibrant colors and borders that will enhance and highlight the text.

ASSESSMENT

✓ Did the student participate in the class discussion?

✓ Did the student contribute to the group?

✓ Did the group's bumper sticker make a strong statement or ask a provocative question?

✓ Did the group devise a bumper sticker caption that was clear and concise?

✓ Did the group use fonts, colors, and other design elements that draw attention to their bumper sticker captions?

Candy Bar Wrapper

PREPARE

Prepare: Collect candy bar wrappers from your family, friends, or your own purchases (yum!) and bring them to class to share with your students.

DISCUSS

Discuss: Pass the candy bar wrappers around to your students and ask them to identify the different types of information featured on the wrappers, such as the candy bar name, main ingredients, nutritional data, special product offers, etc. Then, talk about where this information appears on the wrappers and whether or not text placement is the same on all the candy bar wrappers. For instance, do students find that nutritional information is commonly found on the front or back of a candy bar wrapper?

Next, allow students to vote for the most visually appealing wrapper out of the samples you brought to class (remind students that they are voting for the best wrapper, not candy bar). Discuss the physical characteristics that lead students to deem one wrapper more attractive than another, like the font sizes, styles, and colors used or unique product design and layout. Finally, note the use of any descriptive words, phrases, or adjectives on the wrappers that appeal to the reader's sense of taste ("chocolatey," "sweet," "nutty," "chewy," etc.). Also, note the length of the average candy bar and explain that the text included on a wrapper must fit within the limited space provided.

Writing skill: Be concise and descriptive
This exercise challenges young writers to both inform and persuade readers through the use of descriptive adjectives and short, precise language. Also, as students practice designing visually attractive candy bar wrappers, they learn how important packaging is to the appeal of a product.

Candy Bar Wrapper

WRITE

Write: Students will brainstorm ideas for a new candy bar and compose text for its wrapper. Candy bar concepts can be wacky, like a candy bar made of Brussels sprouts or bugs, or something more traditional, like a mixture of the student's favorite sweets. Students' wrappers should feature the name of the candy bar and a few descriptive words (e.g., "CHOCO-MONGUS—The hunk of junk"), as well as nutritional information, main ingredients, and one other "special info" item of the student's choosing, such as a prize coupon or website address. In addition, instruct students to use descriptive yet concise language that will attract potential consumers.

DRAW

Draw: Students will now create full-color, mock candy bar wrappers that feature the text they composed in the "Write" portion of the exercise. Wrappers can be made out of construction paper and students may use the wrappers you brought to class as templates for their own designs. Or, you can allow students to draw the layout and design of their wrappers to scale on graph paper. Challenge students to use attractive or eye-catching font styles and colors that will garner attention.

ASSESSMENT

✓ Did the student participate in the class discussion?

✓ Was the student able to brainstorm an original candy bar idea?

✓ Did the student include the required information on the wrapper?

✓ Was the student able to create an original layout and design for the wrapper?

✓ Did the physical wrapper display all the information the student wrote for the "Write" portion of this exercise?

✓ Did the student create a full-color wrapper featuring eye-catching font styles and colors?

Captions

PREPARE

Prepare: Cut out several dozen photos from old newspapers and/or magazines that are rich in visual content (e.g., tornado devastation, a rescue scene, an action-packed sports image, etc.), but do not include the explanatory captions that accompany the images. Also, gather a few copies of your local paper to bring to class along with the photos. Distribute at least one photo to each student.

DISCUSS

Discuss: Allow students to study the photos, instructing them to pay close attention to the people in the images. Encourage students to look for visual clues that might reveal location or season, as well as the ages and social status of the people featured in the photos. Also, discuss any emotions captured in the photos (e.g., fear, anger, sadness, joy, anticipation, impatience, confusion, etc.). Then, challenge students to brainstorm several possible scenarios that could explain what is happening in their pictures and encourage volunteers to share their descriptions with the class.

Next, pass around sections of the newspapers you brought to class and ask students to read the captions that appear underneath newspaper photographs. Point out how the caption writer condenses the content of the image in just a few words. Finally, see if students can identify any descriptive details included in the captions and explain that, because photographs freeze an event or scene in time, caption writers must limit their descriptions to what is happening within the frame.

Writing skill: Describing an image
This activity challenges students to inform readers by interpreting and describing visual information. As young writers practice writing explanatory captions, they learn to analyze or "read" images for details that will clarify what a photograph has captured. This exercise, then, develops the visual literacy skills necessary for students learning to inform through description.

Captions

WRITE

Write: Students will write short, one-to two-sentence captions that summarize the action or event captured in their photos for newspaper readers. Students' first drafts will almost certainly be too wordy, so tell them to edit their re-writes ruthlessly. Additionally, encourage students to avoid vague or unspecific language that fails to explain or clarify the photo.

For example, under the image of an automobile accident, a student might write, "Old dude gets busted up in a car wreck." That caption uses slang and provides no descriptive details. Advise students to use language that reflects both the tone of the image and the medium of communication.

DRAW

Draw: Now students will draw an image that depicts the action or event described in a written caption. You can write a caption on the chalkboard or overhead that all students can work from. Student drawings do not have to be complex—stick figures are fine. The idea is simply to visually communicate the action described in the text.

ASSESSMENT

✓ Did the student participate in the class discussion?

✓ Was the student able to write a caption that is no longer than two sentences?

✓ Do the captions provide an accurate description of what appears in the image?

✓ Did the student provide specific, descriptive details that clarify what is happening in the photo?

✓ Did the student make an effort to draw a picture that visually interprets the written caption you provided?

Catalog Information

PREPARE

Prepare: Collect several mail-order catalogs that vary in terms of the products advertised, the intended audience, and the illustrations or photos featured, and bring them to class. Then, distribute a catalog to each student so they can flip through them and read product descriptions.

DISCUSS

Discuss: Ask students to name any adjectives the catalog writers use to describe items. Also, have students count the number of words or sentences that appear in product descriptions. Challenge them to identify the different kinds of information provided in catalog descriptions, such as price, model numbers, sizes, and available colors, as well as any categories dividing products into different sections ("Men," "Women," "Kids," "Repair," "Home," "Maintenance," etc.).

Next, discuss the layout and design of the catalogs, including the use of certain font styles or colors, and why some of the text may appear in bold or large type. Point out any organizational techniques common to catalog layout, such as bullet points to list product features. Do students find that the catalog layouts change from page to page or remain consistent throughout?

Writing skill: Describing a product
In order to write effective catalog copy, students must understand the product they're writing about and be able to describe the product's characteristics, features, and benefits. This exercise will strengthen students' descriptive writing skills while encouraging them to be more "economical" with their language.

Catalog Information

WRITE

Write: Working in small groups, students will pick a product from a catalog and create catalog pages describing that item. Each catalog page must include basic product information, such as model numbers, available colors, and prices. Also, students should be able to identify and highlight any features and benefits unique to the product. Encourage groups to come up with a list of adjectives to use in their product descriptions, and enforce a sentence or word limit that corresponds to standard catalog copy length.

DRAW

Draw: Groups will create an original layout for their catalog page that features drawings of various product views. Tell students to experiment with different font sizes and styles, colors, and bullet points to organize information visually. Students should not use clip art or photos, but they can refer to photographs of real products as "models" for their own art.

ASSESSMENT

✓ Did the student participate in the class discussion?

✓ Did the student contribute to the group?

✓ Does the catalog page accurately describe the product?

✓ Does the catalog page include all the required information?

✓ Did the group create an original layout for their catalog page that features various product views, as well as interesting font styles and colors?

Classified Advertisement

PREPARE

Prepare: Collect the classified sections from several days' newspapers and bring them to class. Then, distribute one or more pages from the classified section to each student and have them study the information that appears in the ads.

DISCUSS

Discuss: First, ask students to identify the basic information provided in the classified advertisements, such as item description, price, and contact information. Instruct students to count the number of words that appear in the ads and then refer them to the advertising rates published in the newspaper. Can students figure out how much it cost to run one of these ads?

Next, allow students to evaluate the ads and determine which ones are the most effective and why. Did ineffective ads leave out important information, or do more appealing ads include a picture of the item for sale? Also, point out the use of any language intended to motivate the reader, such as "Special Offer!" or "Call today!" and talk about the effect of exciting or energizing readers when trying to promote or sell an item.

Writing skill: Motivate your audience
This activity challenges students to write classified ads that are short, descriptive, informative, and motivational. Since words cost money in this exercise, students will practice condensing and editing their writing to highlight only an item's most important or attractive features.

Reaching the Reluctant Writer

Classified Advertisement

WRITE

Write: Students will choose a personal belonging, like an old coat or bicycle, and create a classified ad to sell the item. To emphasize the importance of concise writing in this exercise, tell students that ads cost $1 per word and that they have $25 to spend on the ad. Therefore, students must write their ad in twenty-five words or less. As an added incentive to use words carefully, tell your students that they can keep any money they do not spend (you can use Monopoly™ dollars or any other kind of "play" money). Then, kids can use their extra money to "purchase" stickers, candy, or other small treats from you.

Ads must describe the item, inform readers of its features and price, and motivate potential buyers to purchase the product. It's not okay for a student to write "Bike for sale," and assume he has only spent $3 and may keep the remaining $22. If possible, allow students to enter their ads into a word processing program and print them out in a newspaper format to post in a class or school newspaper.

DRAW

Draw: Students can include an illustration of the item for sale to appear alongside their classified ads. These should be simple black-and-white line drawings that give the reader an idea of the size, dimensions, or model type of the item. In addition, encourage students to experiment with elements of design and layout to create an ad that stands out from others.

ASSESSMENT

✓ Did the student participate in the class discussion?

✓ Did the student stay within the twenty-five-word limit?

✓ Was the student's ad descriptive and informative?

✓ Did the student's ad motivate readers to buy the item?

✓ Did the student attempt to illustrate the item?

Directions

PREPARE

Prepare: Collect free maps from local banks, state rest areas, real estate companies, or state tourism departments and bring them to class. Then, schedule time with the library media specialist for students to study any atlases or maps available at your school's library. If possible, give students time to look at websites that will help them locate their neighborhoods or houses on a map.

DISCUSS

Discuss: Challenge students to identify instances in which maps are necessary or useful, and to share any experiences they have had giving directions to a specific location. Next, talk about what elements are common to clear, well-written directions. Do students find it easier to follow directions that specify landmarks or street names? Do directional terms (e.g., "left," "right," "center," "under," etc.) and commands (e.g., "turn the knob," "look to your right," "count three street lights," etc.) also help clarify written directions?

Last, discuss the visual elements typically included in maps, like a compass, legend, arrows to indicate the direction of travel, or an "X" that marks the spot. Draw a map on the board to a familiar location, such as the school library or cafeteria, and challenge students to identify that location. Then, allow students to offer any suggestions that might make your map easier to read and understand.

Writing skill: Using clear and specific language
Young writers often make the mistake of using vague or ambiguous language that they assume their readers will understand ("stuff," "things," "a long way," "a lot," etc.) rather than words that create specific images in the reader's mind. This exercise will challenge students to make specific, precise word choices in order to direct a reader to an unfamiliar location.

Directions

WRITE

Write: Students will write directions to "mystery" destinations they choose, using your classroom as the starting point. Directions should include at least five steps and reference specific landmarks or street names. Remind students to include distance information, such as "Walk twenty-five steps to the cafeteria door," or "Travel approximately one mile," that might help their readers reach the intended location. Students should assume that their readers are completely unfamiliar with the destination or surrounding area.

DRAW

Draw: Students will now draw maps that show the way to their mystery destinations. Maps should indicate the direction of travel with arrows or dotted lines and include at least three labeled landmarks. Encourage students to provide a "You are here" marker to identify the starting point and an "X" to indicate the destination, as well as a compass to designate cardinal directions.

ASSESSMENT

✓ Did the student participate in the class discussion?

✓ Did the student include at least five steps in the directions?

✓ Are the student's directions clear and unambiguous?

✓ Did the student assume that the reader is totally unfamiliar with the destination?

✓ Did the student's map indicate cardinal directions, starting point, destination, and direction of travel?

Evaluation

PREPARE

Prepare: Collect written claims by politicians, product claims on items in the grocery store, or weight-loss claims from ads in magazines. Once you've gathered a variety of such claims, bring them to class and distribute one to each student. Then, compose a declarative statement about a topic your students will be familiar with and write it on the chalkboard or overhead. For example:

> *Baseball is the best of all sports because:*
> - *It's the most popular game in the world.*
> - *It's played in the warmest part of the year.*
> - *Boys and girls can both play it.*
> - *Nobody ever gets hurt playing baseball.*
> - *Baseball players make a lot of money and that means they're smart.*

DISCUSS

Discuss: Allow students to read the statement and discuss whether they think it reflects a fact or an opinion. Encourage students to share any personal or widely accepted knowledge that might support or refute the above claim, such as knowing a friend who was hurt playing baseball or referencing research that identifies soccer as the most popular game in the world. Next, ask the class to evaluate the claim based on three criteria: 1) *validity* (Is it true?), 2) *clarity* (Is the statement easy to comprehend?), and 3) *motivation* (What outcome does the writer/speaker hope to achieve by making this claim?).

Once enough students have commented, ask them why statements or claims might be evaluated based on validity, clarity, and motivation. Then, see if students can identify any other argumentative statements and claims they hear or see on a daily basis (e.g., print or television advertisements, product claims, celebrity endorsements, campaign speeches, etc.). Do they think these claims offer opinions or facts?

Writing skill: Critique a claim

This exercise will give students an opportunity to evaluate the claims made by other writers/speakers and decide whether or not those claims are valid, clear, and statements of fact or statements designed to motivate. Evaluating the effectiveness or ineffectiveness of other claims bolsters the critical thinking and reading skills students need to become thoughtful, self-aware writers. This exercise, then, will help students recognize when they are making broad generalizations, asserting opinion instead of fact, and exaggerating or over-simplifying an issue.

Evaluation

WRITE

Write: Students will prepare written evaluations of the claims you provided them with. Evaluations should include three complete sentences, one each to address the validity, clarity, and motivation of the claim. Remind students to draw on their own experiences or knowledge when evaluating the statements. Also, instruct students to provide one to two sentences that clearly explain whether they support or refute the claim.

DRAW

Draw: Students can design pocket checklists on three-by-five-inch index cards that display the validity, clarity, and motivation criteria. Encourage students to pull out their pocket checklists to evaluate the claims and arguments they hear on a daily basis, such as celebrity product endorsements, movie reviews, an argument between siblings or kids on the playground, etc. In addition, allow students to add fun cartoons or illustrations to the cards that will help them remember what validity, clarity, and motivation mean.

ASSESSMENT

✓ Did the student participate in the class discussion?

✓ Did the student reference the validity, clarity, and motivation criteria in the evaluation?

✓ Has the student taken a position regarding the claims and explained that position?

✓ Is the student's evaluation of the claim clearly written and easy to read?

✓ Has the student offered any personal insight or accurate research to support or refute the claim?

✓ Did the student create a pocket checklist that can be used to evaluate the validity, clarity, and motivation of other arguments or claims?

Features and Benefits

PREPARE

Prepare: Cut out product ads from magazines and newspapers, or record radio and television commercials and bring them to class. Distribute any print ads to students and let them watch or listen to the audio/visual material you taped.

DISCUSS

Discuss: Once students have viewed or listened to the sample ads, identify and discuss the difference between the "features" and "benefits" of the products and services advertised. Explain that features are the factual information about an item, such as the product's size, function, and color, while benefits are the ways in which the buyer will be enriched by the purchase of a product. For example, a sixty-four-ounce container would be a feature of a bottle of laundry detergent while the benefit would be that the larger size saves buyers additional trips to the grocery store.

Next, talk about how the benefits of a product may change depending on a buyer's wants and needs. For example, teachers may purchase a book because it benefits their instructional needs while general readers might choose the same book for its entertainment value alone. To illustrate this point, pick random objects in your classroom and ask students to identify the features of each item. Then, challenge the class to brainstorm various benefits that could be attributed to the objects depending on a buyer's gender, age, occupation, hobbies, or interests. How might these different benefits affect the way a product is advertised?

Invite a speaker: Ask a parent who works in advertising to explain how advertisers write copy that emphasizes a product's features and benefits.

Writing skill: Writing to address a reader's wants and needs
In this exercise, students must identify the wants and needs of a specific audience or demographic and then practice addressing those demands in their writing. Thus, young writers will have to highlight product features and benefits that can fulfill their imagined readers' wants and needs. The ability to identify and address an audience is a valuable skill for students, who must learn to understand their readers in order to effectively inform and persuade them.

Features and Benefits

WRITE

Write: Each student will list at least three features and benefits of some object that you assign to them (compact disc player, video game, type of candy, shoes with Velcro™ straps, etc.). Encourage students to identify a specific target audience that would be interested in buying the product and to create their list of benefits based on the imagined wants and needs of this audience. Target audiences can reflect an age group or people with certain hobbies, special interests, technological skills, clothing styles, etc.

DRAW

Draw: For a humorous twist, students can list their personal features and benefits on two separate sheets of paper. Students may then tape "features" to the front of their shirts and "benefits" to the back. For example, a student who is tall may have "I am tall" listed on the front of her shirt and a statement like "Being tall makes it easier for me to play basketball" on the back side of the shirt. Features and benefits should be neutral or positive, not negative. In addition, challenge students to include sketches or spot art that depict the features and benefits they've listed.

If practical, ask students in advance to bring in old, white T-shirts with no words or images on them. Then allow students to create personalized shirts that display their features and benefits directly on the cloth with black or colored markers.

ASSESSMENT

✓ Did the student participate in the class discussion?

✓ Did the student demonstrate an understanding of the difference between a feature and a benefit?

✓ Did the student identify at least three features and three benefits for the product assigned?

✓ Did the student identify a target audience for the product and devise a list of features and benefits that would fulfill that audience's perceived wants or needs?

✓ Did the student list personal features and benefits and include spot art or sketches on the personalized T-shirt?

Graphic Information

PREPARE

Prepare: Collect graphs from newspapers, magazines, textbooks, and other documents and distribute one to each student. If they are not already familiar with graphs, use these samples to introduce the class to bar graphs, pie charts, and line graphs.

DISCUSS

Discuss: Once students have looked over the graphs, ask them to identify the data that is presented in the graphs. Moreover, can your students interpret and explain what the graphs illustrate (e.g., an increase in the number of births per year from 1950-1954, a continued decrease in the population of an endangered species over the last decade, etc.)? Then, discuss the purpose of displaying information graphically, explaining that graphs help readers comprehend trends, or data collected over a specific period of time.

Writing skill: Presenting information graphically

In this exercise, students will learn how images can be used to communicate information quickly to readers. By "translating" graphical information into words, young writers become more proficient at description and explanation. This activity also gives students the opportunity to draw larger conclusions based on graphical information, a skill which further develops visual literacy.

Graphic Information

WRITE

Write: Each student will write text that explains the visual information represented in the graphs you provided them with. Encourage students to describe the graphic information clearly and comprehensively to clarify what the graph illustrates. Also, challenge students to draw conclusions based on their written interpretations of the graphs (e.g., what does the graph tell them?).

DRAW

Draw: Now, provide each student with textual descriptions of data from which they will draw graphs. You can write the information yourself or you can acquire statistical information from newspapers, magazines, books, and almanacs. Students should appropriately label their graphs to ensure clarity and comprehension.

You can also read data aloud to students as a narrative and ask them to create a graph of what you read. Students should use one of the graphic formats referred to in the "Prepare" section, but encourage them to experiment with different types of graphs (line graphs, bar graphs, pie charts) to figure out which one most clearly and effectively represents the information provided.

ASSESSMENT

✓ Did the student participate in the class discussion?

✓ Was the student able to describe the graph clearly and accurately in words?

✓ Was the student able to draw any conclusions based on the graphical information?

✓ Was the student able to graphically represent the textual information you provided?

✓ Did the student create a graph that is clearly drawn and labeled?

Greeting Cards

PREPARE

Prepare: Save or collect birthday, holiday, and inspirational greeting cards and bring them to class. Also, explain the concept of word play to your students, identifying how the use of puns, rhymes, alliteration, and clichés can render more humorous or memorable texts.

DISCUSS

Discuss: Once students have looked over the different types of greeting cards you brought in, ask if they can identify a greeting card "format" or any other stylistic elements common to the different cards. Then, point out that humorous greeting cards typically follow a specific format, in which the text on the front of the card acts as a "set-up" and the inside text presents the "punch line."

Next, ask students if they notice any uses of word play, such as puns, rhymes, alliteration, or clichés in the humorous cards. Do they think these examples of word play make the card more humorous or memorable? Finally, urge the class to look at the illustrations inside the greeting cards and note how the style of artwork reflects the tone of the greeting card. For instance, do students think silly, "cartoonish" drawings are more likely to appear in a sympathy card or a birthday greeting?

Writing skill: Practicing word play
In this exercise, students practice using various forms of word play to create clever set-ups and punch lines for humorous greeting cards. As students infuse their writing with wit and humor, they develop personal writing voices that will engage and amuse readers.

Reaching the Reluctant Writer

Greeting Cards

WRITE

Write: Students will compose the text for humorous greeting cards following the "set-up and punch line" format noted in the "Discuss" section. The card can be for any typical occasion, like a birthday or holiday, or students can "think funny" and create greeting cards for an unusual occasion, such as "Sorry you have so much homework" or "Congratulations, I heard your hamster had babies!" Encourage students to use puns, clichés, alliteration, rhyming, or some other form of word play in an effort to make their card humorous.

DRAW

Draw: Students should illustrate their greeting cards with original artwork. Challenge them to study the greeting cards you've brought to class for ideas regarding innovative layout and eye-catching design elements, such as borders, spot art, interesting fonts, and attractive colors. Remind students that their artwork can be a source of humor, and urge them to try drawing exaggerated or ridiculous cartoons that reinforce the punch lines they have written.

ASSESSMENT

✓ Did the student participate in the class discussion?

✓ Did the student follow the "set-up on the outside and a punch line on the inside" format?

✓ Did the student attempt to use humor in the greeting card?

✓ Did the student incorporate any forms of word play, such as puns, rhymes, alliteration, or clichés, in the text of the card?

✓ Did the student's illustration of the card complement the text or add humor to the greeting card?

✓ Did the student create an original layout and design for the card that included attractive fonts and colors?

Grocery List

PREPARE

Prepare: Begin by giving students time outside of class to prepare lists of all the different foods their families typically eat in a week (an adult will probably have to help them with this task). Also, tell students to estimate the amount of food the family eats during that time period (e.g., two boxes of cereal, a dozen eggs, one carton of ice cream, etc.). Finally, ask students to prepare separate lists of ingredients for at least one of their favorite family meals or recipes and to observe the time and preparation involved in creating these dishes.

DISCUSS

Discuss: Once students have completed their lists, discuss the different kinds of food their families like to cook and eat, and whether or not they were surprised by the amount of food their families consumed in a week. Then, invite students to share how their parents or guardians prepare to buy a week's worth of food and if they make lists before leaving for the grocery store. Then, talk about the purpose of list-making and how lists can help one identify and organize ideas, plans, and necessary materials before beginning a project. Can students think of any other instances in which lists might be helpful, such as preparing to write a term paper or conducting a science project?

Writing skill: List-making
This exercise requires the ability to think sequentially and identify the component parts necessary for fulfilling a specific task. When students create lists, they are forced to think through an entire project by mapping it out from start to finish. List-making is a foundational skill for young writers who must learn to organize their thoughts before expanding them into longer written texts.

Reaching the Reluctant Writer

Grocery List

WRITE

Write: Students will create grocery lists of the items needed to prepare a special meal. Examples could include favorite family recipes, vegetarian meals, or various ethnic dishes. Students can also create lists for a special occasion or event, such as a birthday party or Thanksgiving dinner. Encourage the students to think through the entire preparation of the meal or event in order to create a comprehensive and effective list. Students' lists should include a minimum of ten items.

DRAW

Draw: Students can translate their written lists into graphic lists. In other words, instead of writing the word "milk" or "bread" on the list, students may draw a container of milk or a loaf of bread. These can be simple, black-and-white line drawings or more detailed, colored spot art.

Students can also display their grocery lists in a "checklist" format that features small boxes next to each item that users can "check off" as they go down the list. Allow students to decorate their checklists with borders, spot art, and attractive fonts.

ASSESSMENT

✓ Did the student participate in the class discussion?

✓ Was the student's shopping list appropriate for the meal or occasion?

✓ Did the student pick a meal or event that required at least ten items?

✓ Was the student's list complete (you can poll the class for other items the student may have forgotten)?

✓ Did the student attempt to represent the list items graphically with spot art or create a functional checklist format?

Headlines

PREPARE

Prepare: Cut out numerous newspaper articles from your local paper that are developmentally appropriate for your class's grade and skill level. Be sure to include headlines with the articles you collect and distribute two articles to each student in your class.

DISCUSS

Discuss: Let students read the first and last paragraphs from the two articles you provided and ask volunteers to give a one-to two-sentence summarization of what their articles are about. Then, direct the class's attention to the headlines that appear above their articles. Do the students notice any writing elements common to their two headlines? Ask students to count the number of words in each headline and identify the different parts of speech used. In addition, point out that headlines do not always form complete sentences and that grammatical articles like "a," "an," and "the" are often removed in the interest of space.

Next, discuss the content of the headlines and whether or not students think the headlines effectively summarize the articles. Explain that headlines are essentially condensed versions of articles and that their purpose is to inform the reader in as few words as possible. Finally, ask the class if anyone has a humorous headline or a headline that features some form of word play, such as rhymes, puns, or clichés. Do students think humorous headlines attract more readers than serious headlines?

Writing skill: Summarizing information
In this exercise, young writers will practice choosing the most important information from a passage of text and concisely transforming that information into a headline. Students will also have an opportunity to use word play and humor to make their headlines more interesting or appealing to readers.

Reaching the Reluctant Writer

Headlines

WRITE

Write: Students will write alternative headlines for the two articles you provided them with. Headlines should be no more than seven words and should adequately summarize the content of the articles. You can encourage the use of puns, rhymes, alliteration, and other forms of word play, but remind students that headlines must accurately represent the content of the articles. For example, an original headline that reads "New City Sewer System Has Many Problems" could be rewritten as "New City Sewer System Stinks."

DRAW

Draw: Students can illustrate their revised headlines using clever lettering or creative spot art. For instance, a headline about an outbreak of chicken pox could be drawn with letters that have small red dots on them. Instruct students to cut the original headline off their article and glue or tape the article onto a piece of white paper. Now students can display their alternative headlines above each article.

ASSESSMENT

✓ Did the student participate in the class discussion?

✓ Did the student's headlines accurately summarize the articles?

✓ Did the student write alternative headlines in seven words or less?

✓ Did the student incorporate any humor or word play into the alternative headlines?

✓ Did the student display the alternative headlines in a clever or creative way?

How-to Instructions

PREPARE

Prepare: Schedule class time with your school's library media specialist so your students can browse through some instructional, or "how-to," books. If possible, allow students to research how-to books on the Internet.

DISCUSS

Discuss: First, ask students to name the different kinds of how-to books they researched or viewed and whether or not they found them interesting or useful. Based on their observations, what elements make an effective how-to book? Then, urge students to study the organizational layout and graphics used in their how-to texts, including numbered lists, bullets, varying fonts, and diagrams. Can the class identify the purpose of diagrams in instructional texts?

Next, explain that many textbooks are how-to books in that they define a concept or idea and then show students how to use it. Allow students to take a look at their math textbooks and identify how the textbook writers explain mathematical concepts to readers. Moreover, ask the class to pay attention to how the textbook is written, noting the use of simple versus complex sentences, precise wording, and clear language. Can students explain why this style of writing might be helpful when teaching students complicated concepts?

Writing skill: Writing for clarity and specificity
Writing clear and specific instructions is the goal of this exercise. Students must be precise in their word choice to avoid ambiguity and specific when relating their step-by-step instructions. For instance, young writers will learn the difference between a command that reads "Turn and lift your arm" and a more specific statement like "Turn to your left and lift your right arm straight up above your head."

How-to Instructions

WRITE

Write: Students will choose activities they can do well and write step-by-step instructions explaining how to perform those tasks. The activity can be as simple as making a peanut butter and jelly sandwich, or as complicated as snowboarding or repairing a bicycle. Students should assume that their readers know nothing about the topic and strive for clarity and specificity in their instructions.

DRAW

Draw: Students will create illustrations or diagrams that clarify the step-by-step processes they have described. Also, instruct students to draw each step of the task on separate pages to fashion a how-to booklet. Illustrations must be referenced in the instructional text, and students should include drawings that "zoom in" to show close-up diagrams of each step.

ASSESSMENT

✓ Did the student participate in the class discussion?

✓ Did the student write the how-to instructions in a step-by-step format?

✓ Did the student include illustrations?

✓ Are the illustrations or diagrams referred to in the text?

✓ Would a reader unfamiliar with the how-to activity the student described feel empowered to attempt the task?

Interview

PREPARE

Prepare: Search newspapers and magazines for interviews with celebrities and/or professional athletes that include photographs. Pick two of the most interesting or dynamic interviews and make copies of each to distribute to the entire class.

DISCUSS

Discuss: First, challenge students to identify the different types of information they expect to learn about the subject of a newspaper or magazine interview, and list students' suggestions on the chalkboard or overhead. Then, encourage the class to brainstorm a series of questions that an interviewer might pose to a subject based on the information displayed on the board.

Next, explain that interview questions may vary depending on the person being interviewed and the form of publication in which the interview will appear. For instance, does the class think an interviewer would ask a political figure and an entertainment celebrity the same questions? Likewise, how might the interviews in a teen magazine differ from those in a newspaper?

Last, direct the class's attention to the photos of interview subjects that accompany the magazine or newspaper interviews you provided. See if students can describe the tone or mood of the photographs, asking them to note color, lighting, wardrobe, and even the subjects' facial expressions. Explain that photographs typically reflect the tone of an interview as well as the seriousness or silliness of the person being interviewed.

Writing skill: Acquiring and organizing information
In this exercise, students will learn how to acquire information from first sources and then organize that information to create an engaging short interview. In order to write quality non-fiction, young writers must be able to prepare ahead of time and gather all the information they need before they begin writing. By conducting their own interviews, students will practice formulating thoughtful questions that engender equally thoughtful, thorough answers.

Reaching the Reluctant Writer

Interview

WRITE

Write: Students will get in groups of two and interview each other using the questions suggested in the "Discuss" section as guidelines. After you divide the class into pairs, give each student some time before the interview to prepare their questions. Tell students that their interviews can appear in either a magazine or newspaper, and that they should formulate questions that will reflect the tone of the medium they choose.

If possible, try to pair students who don't normally interact. The object is for students to gather new, interesting information about their subjects, and good friends probably know most of this information already. Once students have completed their interviews, they will translate the information gathered about their peers into short, two-to three-paragraph written interviews.

DRAW

Draw: Students can sit opposite one another and draw portraits to include with their interviews. Encourage students to embellish their drawings. For instance, a student who aspires to be an actor can be drawn on a stage, or a student who enjoys soccer could be illustrated holding a soccer ball. Bind all the interviews and drawings together as a "class biography" and put it in a prominent place in the classroom for students to view.

ASSESSMENT

✓ Did the student participate in the class discussion?

✓ Did the student actively participate in the interview?

✓ Did the student formulate thought-provoking interview questions that were appropriate for a newspaper or magazine?

✓ Did the student learn something new or interesting about the person interviewed?

✓ Did the student make a good faith attempt to draw a portrait of the person interviewed?

✓ Did the student embellish the interview subject's portrait in any way?

Invitation

PREPARE

Prepare: Collect a variety of invitations for different events, such as wedding, birthday, graduation, or grand opening celebrations. You can also ask a local print shop to give you free samples of invitations. Bring the invitations you collect to class and allow students to look at them.

DISCUSS

Discuss: First, challenge students to identify all the information provided in the sample invitations. Do students think all invitations follow the same format, or does the class notice any variation in the information featured and how it is displayed? Also, point out any interesting additions to the invitations, such as special notes that specify attire or inform the guest to bring something to the event. Then, explain that a good invitation is comprehensive, meaning that the host must answer any questions that the guest may have within the space provided on the invitation.

Next, ask students to look at the font sizes and styles used in the sample invitations, as well as any borders or spot art, and talk about how these visual details suggest the nature of the event. For instance, what font style would students expect to find in a wedding invitation or an invitation to a pool party?

Invite a speaker: Ask a local wedding planner or printing company rep to talk to your class about the difference between a dynamic and a dull invitation.

Writing skill: Inform your reader
This exercise challenges young writers to create attractive invitations that inform readers about an upcoming event. Besides the usual info regarding time, place, and occasion, students should answer any additional questions that may apply to their made-up event, such as attire or theme. Also, students will develop an overall "look" for their invitations that complements the formality or informality of the occasion.

Invitation

WRITE

Write: Students will write an invitation for some unusual or outrageous event. They may use one of the following examples, or create an event of their own.

- "Come watch me get the cast removed from my broken arm" party
- "Help me clean up my room" celebration
- "Let's watch the grass grow" marathon
- "Please give us more homework" rally (don't expect a big turnout for this one!)

Invitations should identify the name or purpose of the event, the host, date, time, location, RSVP info, and any relevant special notes (e.g., "Bring your bathing suit"). Instruct students to choose language that reflects the formality or informality of their event, and encourage the use of humor or word play if appropriate to the occasion. Invitations should demonstrate that the student has entertained and answered all possible questions the guest/reader may have about the event.

DRAW

Draw: Students will create an original layout and design for their invitations using graphics and font styles that reflect the tone of their made-up event. As always, hand-drawn artwork is preferable, but for this exercise, you may want to allow students to experiment with computer-generated text and graphics.

ASSESSMENT

✓ Did the student participate in the class discussion?

✓ Did the student create an invitation for a truly unusual event?

✓ Did the student include all the required information in the invitation?

✓ Did the artwork and design of the invitation reflect the formality or informality of the student's event?

Jargon

PREPARE

Prepare: First, collect samples of "formal" English, technical jargon, or bureaucratic legalese. You can find examples of such language at local, state, and federal government sites, in insurance policies, privacy statements, or even in the fine print found at the bottom of product offers. Also, gather examples of complicated illustrations, such as assembly instructions for bicycles, furniture, toys, or simple electronics. Bring in at least one example of written jargon and a complex diagram or illustration for each student.

DISCUSS

Discuss: Once the students have read through the samples you collected, read the following sentence aloud to the class:

"Henceforth, while in the passageways during instructional interim periods, it would behoove you to ambulate in a manner commensurate with established safety procedures."

Read the statement again for your students, but tell them beforehand to listen for any words they recognize. Then, write the sentence on your chalkboard and help the class "translate" the statement into everyday language. When students understand what the sentence means, challenge them to write a clearer, simpler version of the statement, such as "Don't run in the hallway."

Next, see if students can identify any other examples of jargon-filled texts, such as board game instructions or rules, assembly directions, and product illustrations. Discuss when it's appropriate to use "big" words and when it's better to use more common language. For instance, how might the intended audience of a text affect the type of language used? Would a manual written specifically for engineers contain the same language as a set of instructions written for a general audience?

Writing skill: Use appropriate diction
This exercise highlights the importance of diction, or word choice, to relaying information. Students learn when jargon, or "stylized language," is necessary and when it confuses or complicates communication. Young writers will also expand their vocabularies as they attempt to choose language that most clearly conveys information to readers.

Jargon

WRITE

Write: Give students a line from Shakespeare or some other developmentally appropriate example of formal English, and ask them to rewrite the sentence, choosing words that a general audience would readily understand. For example, the Shakespeare line from *Romeo and Juliet* that reads "But soft! What light through yonder window breaks? It is the east and Juliet is the sun" could be rewritten as "Shh! I see a light in that window. It's Juliet and she's so beautiful that she looks like the sun coming up in the morning."

Then reverse the assignment, instructing students to rewrite nursery rhymes or children's songs using "big" words. A student could alter the line "London Bridge is falling down" to read "The bridge in the capital city of England is collapsing." Encourage students to envision a particularly erudite or scholarly audience for this portion of the exercise.

DRAW

Draw: Students will simplify the complicated illustrations you provided them with by redrawing them to eliminate unnecessary or complex details. In addition, instruct students to rewrite and clarify any vague or confusing labels that appear in the diagrams.

ASSESSMENT

✓ Did the student participate in the class discussion?

✓ Was the student able to construct a simple, accessible sentence out of the jargon-filled text?

✓ Was the student able to take simple text and rewrite it using "big" words?

✓ Did the student recognize and remove complicated details from the confusing illustrations?

✓ Did the student rewrite any vague labels in the illustrations to make them clearer or more specific?

Labels

PREPARE

Prepare: Collect a variety of photos and illustrations with labeled parts, such as an image of a plant from a biology book, the automobile parts illustrated in your car's owner's manual, a blueprint of a home, or the illustrations in a geography book. If possible, try to gather a few designer clothing labels that feature a graphic image, as well.

DISCUSS

Discuss: Give students a chance to look over the samples you collected. Focusing first on the labeled photos and illustrations, discuss the purpose of labeling the different parts of an image. In terms of learning and retaining information, do students prefer to study a labeled image or read a series of paragraphs? Next, ask students to describe the language used in the labeled images and to count the number of words that appear in each label. Does the class think the labels clarify or confuse the graphic information displayed? Can they identify what makes an effective label?

Finally, shift the class's attention to the clothing labels you brought in and explain that the purpose of clothing labels is not to inform, but to promote a product. Point out how graphic images are used in clothing labels versus labeled illustrations. Are students more likely to remember a brand name with a designer label? Discuss how this form of labeling might affect the value of an item.

Writing skill: Practicing specificity and branding
This exercise challenges students to understand two common but very different forms of labeling. Young writers will practice using clear, specific language to identify and describe an object's constituent parts, and creating memorable labels to attract readers/consumers. This shift from informative to commercial writing also shows students how one mode of communication can serve multiple purposes.

Labels

WRITE

Write: Students will work in small groups to label the different parts of objects that you provide them with, such as a child's mechanical toy, a radio, or a clock. Give groups ten minutes to label as many parts of the object as they can. Students should write the labels on strips of paper and tape them to the physical object. It's okay if students don't know the technical names for individual parts; just encourage them to be as specific as possible when writing labels.

DRAW

Draw: Small groups will now create their own clothing labels. Students should invent a fictitious designer's name and include a distinctive graphic image on the label. Remind groups that they are designing a label and not clothes. Encourage the use of interesting font sizes, styles, and colors, as well as word play and humor to create a memorable label name.

ASSESSMENT

✓ Did the student participate in the class discussion?

✓ Did the student contribute to the group?

✓ Did the group label at least five parts of the object?

✓ Was the information on the labels accurate and specific?

✓ Did the group design a label that includes a graphic image?

✓ Did the group design a label that includes a fictitious designer name?

✓ Did the group create a truly unique label?

Laws

PREPARE

Prepare: Search online for the American Bill of Rights and print out excerpts to bring to class. Make copies for your students and read some of the Constitutional amendments aloud.

DISCUSS

Discuss: As you read the amendments, stop to define any words or phrases your students have trouble understanding. Explain the role the Bill of Rights plays in American government and ask students to share their thoughts on what the amendments mean.

In addition, see if students can describe the writing style of each amendment, noting the reoccurrence of words or phrases (e.g., "shall," "wherein," "life or limb") that might reference the era in which it was written. Allow students to read the preamble to the Bill of Rights as well, explaining that the preamble identifies the purpose and intent of the Constitutional amendments. Discuss how the Bill of Rights is a document that takes a position and establishes the amendments listed as laws.

Invite a speaker: Invite your mayor or a city councilperson to visit your classroom and explain (simply and briefly) to your students how laws are made in your city. Better yet, if your governor or any state representatives are available, ask them to visit; good photo op for them and a great experience for your kids!

Writing skill: Taking a position
Students must express an opinion, take a position, and defend it energetically in this exercise. Young writers will practice translating their ideals into viable "laws" while working with others to reach a common viewpoint. The ability to state a position on paper is a foundational skill for young writers who will be expected to write lengthier position papers as they advance through school.

Laws

WRITE

Write: Students will work in small groups to create five or more laws they would like to see enacted in their school. Groups should focus on laws that are specific to student life, both at school and away from school. Examples might include no bullying, no crude language, no more than two tests per day, etc. Laws must be a minimum of two to three sentences in length, and students should include a three-to four-sentence preamble establishing the purpose and intent of their laws, as well.

DRAW

Draw: Groups can create scrolls on which to print their laws. Challenge students to print their text in calligraphy or other elegant fonts to make their scrolls more formal or "official-looking."

ASSESSMENT

✓ Did the student participate in the class discussion?

✓ Did the student contribute to the group?

✓ Did the group create laws that reflect real issues of interest to students?

✓ Did the group include a preamble that identifies the purpose of their laws?

✓ Did the group create a scroll and print their laws on the scroll?

Letter to the Editor

PREPARE

Prepare: Gather several letters to the editor from your local newspaper's editorial page over the course of a week. Also, cut out a number of editorial cartoons that lampoon current events. Make copies of the letters and cartoons you've collected and distribute them to your students.

DISCUSS

Discuss: Pick one or two student volunteers to read their letters to the editor aloud, and ask the class to share their first impressions of the letters and the letter writers. Do students agree or disagree with what the writers wrote? Explain that letters to the editor allow people to express their opinions about an issue recently discussed in a newspaper or magazine.

Next, poll the class to see if students think the writers argued their points convincingly or not. Would they change any of the writers' words or arguments to make the letters more powerful or persuasive? Challenge students to identify what a writer should or should not do when presenting an opinion. For instance, is an argument weakened or strengthened when a writer offers supporting evidence to back up a point of view? Likewise, discuss how a writer's tone can affect the credibility and persuasiveness of an argument.

Ask students to look at the editorial cartoons you brought to class. Define the concept of satire or parody to your students and see if they can recognize these elements in their cartoons. Discuss how the cartoons are drawn as well, noting any embellishment or exaggeration in the illustrations. Point out that humor can also be used to express an opinion or state an argument.

Invite a speaker: Invite your local newspaper's editor or editorial cartoonist to class to explain how important the op-ed page is to the free exchange of information.

Writing skill: Presenting and supporting an opinion
In order to write an effective letter to the editor, students will have to express an opinion succinctly, and justify their arguments. Students will learn how to write both fact and opinion in the same letter. This exercise also develops students' ability to write passionately without ranting—a tricky combination for writers of any age.

Letter to the Editor

WRITE

Write: Students will draft "letters to the principal" expressing their thoughts or concerns about school-related issues, citing any personal experiences that may support the opinions they present. For instance, a student letter arguing for a change in cafeteria food could reference more favorable menu options available at other schools. Letters should be addressed to your school's principal and must include a date, salutation, body, closing, and signature.

DRAW

Draw: Challenge students to draw editorial cartoons that reflect the sentiments expressed in their letters to the principal. Students should use metaphors, exaggeration, and humor to visually depict their point of view. For example, a situation that is difficult to resolve at school could be illustrated as Humpty Dumpty, who couldn't be put back together again.

ASSESSMENT

✓ Did the student participate in the class discussion?

✓ Did the student's letter to the principal conform to the conventional letter format?

✓ Did the student make a good faith attempt to draw an editorial cartoon?

✓ Does the editorial cartoon reflect the issue addressed in the student's letter?

✓ Does the student's editorial cartoon use metaphor, exaggeration, or humor to visually express an opinion?

Menus

PREPARE

Prepare: Gather sample menus from a wide variety of local restaurants, including drive-through, upscale, ethnic, and take-out eateries. Bring the menus you collected to class and pass them around for your students to view.

DISCUSS

Discuss: Once students have had the chance to look over each menu, ask them to pick the food items they find most appealing and note any adjectives, adverbs, or metaphors used to describe those items. Encourage students to identify which menu descriptions sound accurate and which seem exaggerated or embellished. Does the class notice that the pricier menus tend to feature more vivid food descriptions?

In addition, discuss the layout and design of the menus, focusing on the colors, font styles, and graphics used in each. Ask students to note how the menu designs differ between expensive restaurants and more casual venues. For instance, are students more likely to see elegant script in the menu for a fancy French restaurant or a pizza parlor? Finally, point out any additional information included on the menus, such as prices and contact information, as well as how different menu options are categorized ("Appetizers," "Entrées," "Desserts," "Kids Menu," etc.).

Invite a speaker: Invite a local restaurateur to your class to discuss how menu items are chosen.

Writing skill: Practicing the use of hyperbole
This activity exercises students' creative writing skills by developing their knowledge and use of adjectives, adverbs, and metaphors. In addition, students can use humor to mimic the hyperbolic writing style characteristic of most menu descriptions. Young writers will find that relying on their sense of humor gives them the freedom to be more outrageous, imaginative, and vivid in their descriptions.

Reaching the Reluctant Writer

Menus

WRITE

Write: Students will work in small groups to create menus for bizarre or outlandish restaurants. "Unusual" restaurants might serve the following:

- Exotic (but not endangered) birds, fish, or reptiles
- Food for creatures from another planet
- Food that only grows underground (yams, peanuts, potatoes, etc.)
- Food that only grows on trees (pecans, oranges, almonds, olives, etc.)
- Road kill (yucky, but funny!)

Descriptions of menu items should include adjectives, adverbs, and metaphors that are "over the top." Here's an example:

"The Armadillo Soufflé Grande is an angelic symphony of the most tender, motor oil-marinated filets of recently demised, worm-fed, free-range armadillo suspended within a moist cloud of air-infused, gravity-defying eggs."

Groups should create at least four menu items and display them in different categories (e.g., one appetizer, one entrée, one dessert, and one kids' menu item). Remind students to provide a restaurant name, contact information, and prices for their menu items.

DRAW

Draw: Each group will create an original layout and design for their menu, including illustrations and attractive fonts. Discourage the use of clip art, but prompt students to lay out their words and graphics in interesting or unusual ways. Menu designs should reflect the formality or informality of their menu descriptions as well.

ASSESSMENT

✓ Did the student participate in the class discussion?

✓ Did the student contribute to the group?

✓ Did the group's menu descriptions include adjectives, adverbs, or metaphors that exaggerated the characteristics of the dish?

✓ Did the group create at least four menu items and include prices, contact information, and a restaurant name on their menu?

✓ Did the group create an attractive menu that included interesting design elements such as unusual font styles and graphics?

Movie Review

PREPARE

Prepare: Cut or photocopy movie reviews from your local newspaper, magazines, or online sources. If possible, try to find both positive and negative reviews for the same movies. Bring the reviews you've gathered to class and share them with your students.

DISCUSS

Discuss: First, encourage students to share whether or not movie reviews influence their decisions to see movies. Are advertisements, trailers, or friends' recommendations more likely to affect the movie choices they make? Explain that movie reviews reflect one writer's point of view, but that a reviewer's opinions should be backed up with evidence that supports why a movie is deemed good or bad.

Next, ask students to brainstorm the supporting details a writer should cite when reviewing a film, such as the quality of the acting, direction, plot, characterization, camera work, etc. Discuss how addressing these elements of the movie can justify the writer's opinion and, in turn, affect the overall persuasiveness of the review. Also, point out any other information that appears in movie reviews, such as the title, running time, leading actors, and a brief summary of the film's plot.

Finally, note any visual ratings systems that accompany the movie reviews you brought in, like a "two thumbs up" graphic or five stars. Would students rather read a movie review or refer to a visual rating? Discuss the difference between a textual and visual review and why some readers might prefer one form over the other.

Writing skill: Validating an opinion using supporting details
In this exercise, students get a chance to express and validate their opinions by citing supporting evidence. As a result, young writers learn the importance of conveying *why* they hold a certain viewpoint as opposed to simply stating what that viewpoint is. Students will find that supporting their opinions bolsters the persuasiveness of their writing.

Movie Review

WRITE

Write: Students will write reviews for movies they have seen citing evidence that supports their opinions. Encourage your students not to settle on their favorite movies, but rather to write about films that have made them angry, tearful, frightened, giggly, or sentimental. Students should write the movie title above their reviews, as well as the film's running time and leading actors. Reviews must include three reasons that back up the student's overall opinion of the movie, as well as a brief, two-to three-sentence synopsis of the film's plot.

DRAW

Draw: Students will create visual ratings for the movies they review. Ask students to avoid obvious choices by thinking funny and being creative. Examples might include boxes of popcorn (one box of popcorn indicates a bad movie, while five boxes mean the movie was excellent) or an odor-meter (a skunk indicates a bad movie, while a bouquet of roses denotes a quality movie). Instruct students to display their graphic ratings next to the movie title on their written review.

ASSESSMENT

✓ Did the student participate in the class discussion?

✓ Did the student's review provide three reasons why the student liked or disliked the movie?

✓ Did the student's review include the movie title, running time, leading actors, as well as a brief synopsis of the plot?

✓ Was the student specific about what was good or bad about the movie?

✓ Did the student create a clever visual rating system to accompany the movie review?

Movie Titles

PREPARE

Prepare: Cut movie ads out of your local newspaper and, if possible, see if your local movie theater will give you any posters or promotional materials for movies that are currently showing. Bring these items to class and share them with your students.

DISCUSS

Discuss: Invite students to share their favorite movies with the class and write the titles they name on your chalkboard or overhead. Then, allow the class to look over the movie titles displayed on the board and ask students to vote on the top three titles listed (remind them that they are voting for the best *titles*, not movies). Discuss why they prefer the titles they chose over others, and whether or not movie titles influence viewers' film choices. Do students find they are more likely to see films with intriguing, silly, or familiar titles?

Next, challenge students to identify the features of a good movie title, like its ability to make a reader laugh, ask questions, or anticipate seeing the movie. Refer to any posters or promotional materials you brought in and discuss the elements of a movie poster. Explain that posters usually display the movie title, the film's leading actors, and a tag line meant to "tease" or capture the reader's interest. Finally, explain that the tone or mood of a film is typically reflected in the colors, images, and fonts used in movie posters, which is why a poster for *The Lord of the Rings* would be very different than a poster for *How the Grinch Stole Christmas*.

Writing skill: Using word play and hooks
This exercise challenges students to create movie titles that will attract potential viewers and "grab" an audience's attention. Young writers will practice using different forms of word play, such as rhyming, alliteration, clichés, and puns to appeal to a reader's sense of humor or intrigue. This activity also gives students an opportunity to write "hooks," or short, punchy text that readers will easily remember.

Movie Titles

WRITE

Write: Students will write alternative titles for at least three movies they have seen. Encourage students to experiment with different forms of word play and verbal "hooks," or catchy titles that will attract the attention of potential moviegoers. Also, remind students that they can draw inspiration from major themes or events in the movie when brainstorming title ideas.

DRAW

Draw: Students will create movie posters for one of the three alternative titles they have written. In the interest of time, you can have the class vote on the top three rewritten titles and allow small groups of students to work on the posters together. Students should use colors, graphics, and fonts that reflect the content or themes of the movies they have chosen.

In addition, posters must display the students' alternative titles, a tag line, and any leading actors featured in the film.

ASSESSMENT

✓ Did the student participate in the class discussion?

✓ Would the student's alternative titles attract potential viewers?

✓ Did the student attempt to use any word play or hooks in the rewritten titles?

✓ Did the student's alternative titles make sense given the content of the movies?

✓ Did the design of the poster reflect the content and genre of the film?

Owner's Manual

PREPARE

Prepare: Round up various owner's manuals for automobiles, computers, home appliances, or lawn equipment, and bring them to class. Pass the manuals around so each student gets a chance to look through them.

DISCUSS

Discuss: Once every student has had a chance to view the different manuals, point out how each one breaks down and organizes information through the use of a table of contents, lists or bullet points, an index, and headings. Ask students to note any additional information included in the manuals as well, such as caution labels, contact information, and labeled diagrams. Then, talk about the benefits of an organized and comprehensive layout, especially in texts that contain an abundance of content.

Next, discuss the writing style featured in the owner's manuals and the importance of using clear, succinct language when writing for a general audience. Explain that most people will not read their owner's manuals from beginning to end, but rather refer to them only when they have problems operating a product. As a result, owner's manuals should be easy to read, navigate, and understand.

Writing skill: Communicating clearly

The ability to anticipate readers' questions and answer them clearly and comprehensively is an important informational writing skill. Since most everyday texts are written for a mass audience, students should learn how an organized layout and accessible writing style can promote effective communication. This exercise will challenge students to adopt a "user-friendly" style that directly addresses readers' questions and concerns.

Owner's Manual

WRITE

Write: Students will work in small groups to write owner's manuals for any common object they use on a daily basis. Instruct groups to divide the work up so that each student works on different sections of the manual. Students should refer to the owner's manuals you brought to class as models and include any additional information found in the manuals, such as caution or warning labels and contact information.

DRAW

Draw: Groups must include drawings in their manuals showing specific parts, different views of the object, arrows indicating direction of movement, or any other information that is best explained graphically. Remind students to label diagrams and pair graphics with explanatory text to make their manuals clear and accessible for readers. Drawings can be simple black-and-white line art or full-color renderings, depending on the time available for this exercise.

ASSESSMENT

✓ Did the student participate in the class discussion?

✓ Did the student contribute to the group by writing at least one section of the owner's manual?

✓ Did the owner's manual include several sections (e.g., assembly, operating instructions, warnings, warranty, troubleshooting, etc.)?

✓ Did the group include drawings in their manual that are easy to comprehend?

Play-by-Play

PREPARE

Prepare: First, make sure you can get a television and a VCR or DVD player for this exercise. View several videos or DVDs of sporting events, such as the Olympics, Super Bowl, NBA Finals, Stanley Cup Finals, or college sports championship games. Cue each video so it opens with some interesting or dynamic action.

DISCUSS

Discuss: Allow students to view a few minutes of action narrated by sports announcers and explain that commentators describe action live or in "real time," which means they cannot use a script. Also, note that through this play-by-play style of commentary announcers not only inform viewers of what is happening on the field but also clarify and explain the action taking place. Based on this observation, ask students if they can identify any similarities between sports commentary and informational writing. In what ways are these two forms of communication alike and different?

Invite a speaker: Invite a local radio or TV sports announcer to class to explain how commentators make live play-by-play announcing interesting.

Writing skill: Informing through improvisation
Many students feel they are better at saying what they're thinking instead of writing, so this oral exercise will give students who are better at verbal communication a chance to use their skills in a more familiar format. On the other hand, better writers will learn how natural speech patterns and rhythms can inform certain written texts. Encourage young orators to practice using analogies, clichés, figures of speech, idioms, metaphors, and hyperbole in this activity.

Reaching the Reluctant Writer

Play-by-Play

WRITE

Speak: Students will work in pairs to improvise play-by-play commentaries of the sports footage you cued up. Before they begin, turn the TV monitor away from the class, mute the sound, and allow each pair of students to view the action briefly before they begin announcing. Then, turn the TV monitor towards the class and re-cue the video to the spot where the action begins. If possible, allow each pair of students to announce for thirty seconds to a minute. Students should also attempt to interact with one another during this exercise. For example, a student commentary could sound something like this:

> *"Wow! Would you look at that guy skate! Have you ever seen a hockey player with more speed, Jennifer?"*

> *"No, Austin, I haven't. And the amazing thing is how well he controls the puck while he's moving so fast."*

In addition, challenge your students to use descriptive words, analogies, exaggeration, clichés, and humor when describing the action onscreen.

DRAW

Draw: Each pair of students should create a "background" for their play-by-play commentary on the chalkboard behind them. Students can make it look as though they are in front of a large crowd of spectators or inside a broadcast booth. If possible, allow students to construct more elaborate backgrounds using poster board, cardboard, sheets, or any other available materials.

ASSESSMENT

✓ Did the student participate in the class discussion?

✓ Did the student accurately describe the onscreen action?

✓ Did the two students attempt to interact with one another?

✓ Was the student able to do the "play-by-play" for the time allotted?

✓ Did the student participate in the drawing or construction of an original background?

Poster

PREPARE

Prepare: Gather out-of-date posters that reflect commercial, informational, philanthropic, or political interests. You can usually find such posters in store windows, on building walls, or attached to street posts. You can also refer to *A Century of Posters* by Martijn F. Le Coultre and Alston W. Purvis (Lund Humphries Pub., 2002) or *Learn About Movie Posters* by Ed and Susan Poole (iGuide Media, Inc., 2003) for additional samples. Once you have collected a variety of posters, bring them to class and show them to your students.

DISCUSS

Discuss: After students have studied the posters, challenge them to classify each poster as informative, persuasive, or motivational. Explain that though these categories may overlap, posters generally aim to inform the public about an issue, persuade consumers to buy something, or motivate people to take some action. As a result, most posters will directly address the reader in order to garner attention. Can students point out any language in the posters that is clearly designed to attract readers?

Then, talk about the images, colors, and fonts used in the posters. Do students think the posters are easy to read and visually appealing? Identify posters as visual statements that are only effective if they catch the eye of a passerby. Posters must feature language and graphics that can convey a message quickly and in some unique or memorable way. Based on this observation, would your students deem the posters you brought in as effective or ineffective?

Writing skill: Writing to inform, persuade, or motivate
In this activity, students practice tailoring their writing to either inform, persuade, or motivate readers. When students write with one of these objectives in mind, they learn how to engage and elicit specific responses or actions from an audience. Young writers will also be challenged to attract readers with their messages since posters rely on forceful language and compelling images to command attention.

Reaching the Reluctant Writer

Poster

WRITE

Write: Students will work in small groups to create posters that either inform (the dangers of smoking), persuade (join our club), or motivate (attend this concert) an audience. Provide the class with any necessary materials, such as markers, construction paper, or poster board. Students should use language that attracts or directly addresses the reader in order to make their messages more powerful or potent.

DRAW

Draw: Students should create a visually appealing layout and design for their posters. Encourage the use of large or bold fonts that will attract attention, as well as interesting colors and images.

ASSESSMENT

✓ Did the student participate in the class discussion?

✓ Did the student contribute to the group?

✓ Did the group's poster inform, persuade, or motivate readers?

✓ Did the poster include text that actively engages and attracts an audience?

✓ Did the group create a visually appealing poster that will garner attention?

Press Release

PREPARE

Prepare: First, collect a variety of press releases from trade magazines, newspapers, and company websites announcing upcoming events, new products, or store openings. Next, find a calendar that marks as many holidays as possible, including "minor" holidays such as Groundhog Day, April Fools' Day, and Mardi Gras. Bring the calendar and press releases to class to share with your students.

DISCUSS

Discuss: Read the press releases aloud to your class and ask students to identify the different information included, such as a date, explanatory headline, contact information, and a brief description of the event. Based on the information provided, can students determine the purpose of a press release? Point out that press releases not only inform readers but also announce and generate interest for some new event.

Once you've discussed press releases with your class, refer to the calendar and ask students to share their favorite holidays. Then, note the different colors, meals, objects, animals, flowers, and traditions associated with the holidays. Can students identify any images popularly associated with certain holidays, such as hearts for Valentine's Day and four-leaf clovers for St. Patrick's Day? Finally, explain that holidays are established for religious, federal, and even commercial reasons to commemorate famous people and events or to celebrate public interests.

Writing skill: Writing to announce and inform
This exercise gives students the opportunity to practice both informative and promotional writing as they announce the creation of a new holiday. Since press releases are meant to create public interest in a new product or event, young writers must describe their holidays in a way that will appeal to and excite readers.

Press Release

WRITE

Write: Students will write press releases announcing the establishment of new holidays they create. Holidays should reflect some personal interest, such as a "No Homework Day," or commemorate a real person or event. At a minimum, press releases should include the following:

- Date
- Headline (e.g., "New Holiday Gives Kids a 'Homework-Free' Day")
- Two-paragraph description of the holiday and why it was established
- Contact information

DRAW

Draw: Challenge students to design buttons to wear in honor of their new holidays. Buttons should include the name of the holiday and a graphic that represents the holiday, such as a pencil with a diagonal line through it for "No Homework Day." Students can create their buttons by cutting circles out of construction paper and taping them to their shirts. You can also purchase small glue-on pins from a craft store and fasten them to the backs of students' buttons so they can be worn.

ASSESSMENT

✓ Did the student participate in the class discussion?

✓ Was the student able to create an original holiday?

✓ Did the student's press release inform readers and promote the new holiday?

✓ Did the student include the required information in the press release?

✓ Did the student design a button that included a symbol or graphic representative of the holiday?

Program

PREPARE

Prepare: Collect programs from various school, musical, theatrical, and sporting events. You can also contact a local printing company for extra copies of programs they have printed. Once you have a variety of programs, bring them to class and pass them around to your students.

DISCUSS

Discuss: Ask students to study the programs carefully, noting the information included as well as the designs and graphics featured. Point out that programs typically offer interesting background information related to the event, such as player stats, actor names and characters, about the author text, and relevant historical data. Then, ask your students to identify why spectators find programs useful.

Finally, allow students to describe the colors and images used in the programs. Do students think the programs are visually appealing? Explain that an effective program stimulates viewer interest through the use of graphics, fonts, and colors representative of the production or event.

Writing skill: Writing to engage and inform
This exercise challenges students to write informational text that also engages and interests readers. Young writers will be expected to expand upon the journalistic form of informational writing (who, what, where, why, when, how) to provide a detailed preview of what spectators will see.

Program

WRITE

Write: Students will create programs for real or fictitious events, such as a school assembly, a birthday party, an awards banquet, a family gathering, a talent show, etc. Programs should include the event title, location, date, and time, as well as the names of event participants, and a list of the activities that will take place. In addition, students must anticipate and answer any questions the reader may have by assuming that their reader has no previous knowledge about the event.

DRAW

Draw: Each student should create an original design and layout for their programs. Encourage the use of appealing fonts, colors, and images that will engage readers and stimulate interest in the event. Also, remind students to include visual elements that reflect the nature of their event.

ASSESSMENT

✓ Did the student participate in the class discussion?

✓ Did the student's program include the required information?

✓ Did the student anticipate and answer any questions the reader might have?

✓ Does the program include participant names and event activities?

✓ Did the student create an original layout for the program that included fonts, colors, and images representative of the event?

Recipes

PREPARE

Prepare: Gather your own cookbooks or borrow some from friends and relatives. Also, cut recipes from newspapers and magazines or print recipes from online sources. Bring the recipes you collected to class and pass them around to your students.

DISCUSS

Discuss: Encourage students to share any recipes they know that include more than two steps ("open box and place in microwave" would not count as a recipe). Then, pick a food item that most students will be familiar with, such as a grilled cheese sandwich, and challenge the class to describe how that food item is made. As students volunteer information, write their comments on the chalkboard in a step-by-step format.

Next, allow the class to read over the steps and edit them for clarity and specificity. For instance, did students specify cooking temperatures, times, or ingredient measurements? Explain that written recipes must be very exact so readers can complete the recipe with ease. Refer students to the recipes you brought in and ask them to identify any other information common to recipes, such as a list of ingredients needed, a brief description of the recipe, and a picture of the end product. Finally, discuss how the recipe directions are written, noting the frequent use of "commanding" verbs (e.g., "*Spread* butter on both sides of the sandwich and *heat* over a skillet for three to five minutes").

Invite a speaker: Invite a local chef to your class to discuss how new recipes are created. Have the chef discuss the importance of math in cooking (measuring, weight, timing, etc.) and the skills necessary to being an accomplished chef.

Writing skill: Practicing clarity and specificity
This exercise challenges students to describe a process logically and sequentially so that readers can successfully perform that task on their own. When young writers are prompted to think through an entire procedure, they must identify and answer any problems, questions, or concerns the reader may encounter. Students learn the importance of writing clear, specific text when they practice writing recipes.

Recipes

WRITE

Write: Students will create cookbooks that feature at least three recipes they know how to prepare. Students should choose recipes that involve a minimum of three steps, but recipes can be as simple as a peanut butter and jelly sandwich or hot chocolate. If possible, allow students to spend one evening working with an adult in the house to help them detail the specific sequencing, measurements, and timing necessary to complete the recipe. Then, have students bring the information they gathered at home to class to finish the assignment. Student cookbooks should include a list of ingredients and a brief description of the food item, and students should use active, or "commanding" verbs to communicate their step-by-step directions.

DRAW

Draw: Students should provide hand-drawn illustrations of the completed recipes in their cookbooks. Encourage your students to make their drawings appear as appetizing as possible, and to present the recipes in fun and creative ways. For example, a student could draw a slice of bread above and below the recipe for a peanut butter and jelly sandwich, so that the recipe is literally "sandwiched."

ASSESSMENT

✓ Did the student participate in the class discussion?

✓ Did the student write at least three recipes?

✓ Did the student include a list of ingredients and a brief description of the food?

✓ Did the student include specific sequencing, measurement, and timing information?

✓ Did the student write clear, complete sentences that featured active verbs?

✓ Did the student provide a drawing of the finished product?

Résumé

Prepare: Gather some sample résumés from online job searches or ask a local job search firm to provide you with résumé information. Also, cut out ads for job offers that appear in the classified section of your local paper. Bring plenty of samples to class and distribute one to each student.

Discuss: Give students time to read over the samples and ask them to name the different headings that appear in the résumés, such as contact info, job objective, education, experience, references, etc. Then, allow students to brainstorm the general qualities most employers seek in an employee, like dependability and experience in a specific field. Explain that a well-written résumé is particularly important because it is the employer's first impression of a potential employee. Based on that observation, do students think a résumé riddled with spelling and grammatical errors would be seriously considered?

Invite a speaker: Invite a job recruiter to your class to discuss how important a solid résumé is to getting a good job.

Writing skill: Conveying an appropriate tone
As students write résumés, they learn how to modify their tone to present information about themselves in a "professional" manner. This exercise also gives young writers an opportunity to "beef up" their résumés with action words that show, rather than tell, how qualified they are. By incorporating action words into their writing, students will see firsthand the importance of word choice—the more appropriate action words they include, the more responsible and capable they sound.

Reaching the Reluctant Writer

Résumé

WRITE

Write: Each student will write a résumé detailing their skills and capabilities. Résumés should include the student's name, address, contact info, job objective, educational background, experience, achievements, hobbies, and references. Provide the class with examples of jobs they can apply for, such as babysitting, yard work, or running a lemonade stand. Students can also write résumés for student council positions, like class president, secretary, and treasurer. Remind them to be specific and use action words when detailing their work experience. For example, a line from a résumé for a babysitting job that reads, "I watch my brother when my Mom and Dad go out," could be improved with action words to read as follows:

"Babysitting – When my Mom and Dad go out, I prepare dinner for myself and my brother, and then I clean up the kitchen. I'm also responsible for making sure my brother takes his bath, brushes his teeth, and gets into bed by 9 p.m."

Students can also create résumés for popular cartoon or television characters. For instance, what experience or references would Cookie Monster have? Likewise, what previous education and skills would Donald Duck bring to a job? This variation on the assignment will give students a chance to develop their creative writing skills by adopting the voices of familiar characters.

DRAW

Draw: Students will present their résumés in an accessible, coherent format using the sample résumés you brought to class as models. Encourage the use of interesting fonts, borders, and spot art to make the résumés visually appealing.

ASSESSMENT

✓ Did the student participate in the class discussion?

✓ Did the student's résumé include all the required information?

✓ Did the student use action words in the "Experience" section of the résumé?

✓ Did the student present information in an organized, accessible layout?

✓ Did the student embellish the résumé with attractive fonts, borders, and spot art?

Rule Book

PREPARE

Prepare: Collect a variety of rule books or instructional manuals from board games that are marketed to adults and children of different ages. Rule books for popular board games are also available online. Once you've gathered a number of rule books, bring them to class for your students to view.

DISCUSS

Discuss: After students have studied the rule books, ask them to name any games they play on a regular basis. Pick one of the games named and work with your students to devise a list of rules for that game. Write students' suggestions on the board, and then challenge your class to identify the object of the game and list any game pieces or tools necessary for play. Can students think of any more information a reader/player should know before playing the game?

Next, refer students back to the sample game rules you brought in and point out the different headings used to organize information, such as "Objective," "Contents," "How to Play," etc. Also, note any variation in writing styles between rule books, explaining that tone and word choice typically depend on the age range of players the game is meant to satisfy. For instance, the audience for a game like Candy Land™ would require a more simplistic rule book than the audience of an adult game like Trivial Pursuit™.

Writing skill: Be clear and comprehensive
This is an exercise in creativity and clarity as students must devise a set of rules that is comprehensive, fun, fair, and easy to understand. In addition, young writers will be expected to tailor their rule books to satisfy the needs and interests of a specific age group.

Reaching the Reluctant Writer

Rule Book

WRITE

Write: Students will work in small groups to create rule books for an invented game. Give groups the freedom to develop any type of game they wish, whether it be a sports game, board game, word game, card game, etc. However, students must create their games for a specific age group, and rule books should be written with that audience in mind. Students should also divide their rule books into different categories detailing the game's objective, contents, and playing instructions. Remind students to strive for clarity in their writing.

DRAW

Draw: Groups can devise original layouts for their rule books and design or create the materials needed to play their invented games. Students may create boards for board games, a deck of cards for card games, or a diagram of a field and player positions for a sports game. Rule books should feature spot art or drawings of player pieces and materials. Artwork and game materials do not have to be elaborate, but the concepts should be creative and carefully planned.

ASSESSMENT

✓ Did the student participate in the class discussion?

✓ Did the student contribute to the group?

✓ Did the group create a workable game?

✓ Were the group's rules clear and comprehensive?

✓ Was the group's rule book divided into the required categories?

✓ Did the group design an original layout for the rule book and create any necessary game materials?

Slang Dictionary

PREPARE

Prepare: Make a list of slang terms that are obsolete or passé, like "keen," "groovy," or "rad." You can find lists of these words online, or you can visit your local library and refer to a slang dictionary. Bring your list, along with a regular, formal dictionary, to class and write your list of slang words on the chalkboard or overhead.

DISCUSS

Discuss: Challenge students to define the dated slang terms you've listed. Then, ask the class to share any slang words they frequently use (barring any offensive words or phrases, of course) and see if students can provide clear definitions for those terms. Ask students if they can pinpoint where and when they first heard these words, and explain that slang is a product of the different values or trends that define a particular culture or generation.

Next, pass around the formal dictionary you brought in and have students study how definitions are written. Note the different types of information provided in a definition, such as pronunciation, part of speech, multiple meanings, sample sentences, word origins, synonyms, etc. Also, point out any illustrations that appear alongside definitions. Do students think the illustrations clarify the meaning of a word?

Writing skill: Defining common terms
This exercise forces students to write clear, detailed definitions of the words they use on a daily basis. By mimicking the style of writing common to dictionary entries, young writers will learn to analyze and intellectualize the meanings and origins of their favorite slang terms.

Slang Dictionary

WRITE

Write: Students will work in small groups to compile a dictionary of popular slang terms. Slang dictionary entries should include the word in bold text followed by its pronunciation, part of speech, a detailed definition, and a sample sentence that illustrates how each word is used. Encourage students to provide any other meanings that may be associated with a word and to assume that their reader is unfamiliar with the slang terms. Each group should compose at least ten entries for their slang dictionaries.

DRAW

Draw: Students can include small cartoons or illustrations to further clarify the slang words or phrases defined. Illustrations should be simple, black-and-white line drawings, but encourage students to create fun or wacky images that will help readers understand and remember the terms.

ASSESSMENT

✓ Did the student participate in the class discussion?

✓ Did the student contribute to the group?

✓ Was the group able to identify at least ten slang words or phrases?

✓ Were the slang definitions clear and comprehensive?

✓ Did the group include cartoons or illustrations to clarify their definitions?

Song Lyrics

PREPARE

Prepare: Search the Internet for the lyrics of current, popular songs that follow tight rhyme schemes. Pick one of the songs and make enough copies of the lyrics to pass around to each student in your class.

DISCUSS

Discuss: Give students a few moments to read over the lyrics on paper, and then encourage the class to sing all or part of the song aloud with you. Write one or two verses from the song on the chalkboard or overhead and ask students to underline all the rhyming words that appear in those verses. Help them identify whether or not the song follows a specific rhyme scheme. Using the verse(s) you copied onto the board, mark the first rhyming lines with an "A," the second with a "B," and so forth. Now, you can classify the song's rhyming pattern as "A A B B," "A B A B," or some other variation.

Next, ask students if they can think of any songs that are repetitive or tend to "stick" in their memory. Country music and "pop" songs are good examples. Explain that most popular songs rely on catchy lyrics or rhythms known as "hooks" that make a song more memorable.

Writing skill: Create a hook using rhyming words
This exercise develops a student's ability to compose catchy or memorable hooks that engage an audience. In addition, this activity cultivates the listening skills that will help students write more rhythmically. As they learn to recognize and recreate basic rhyme schemes, young writers will practice shaping and fine-tuning their writing to fit a specific rhythm or rhyme pattern.

Song Lyrics

WRITE

Write: Small groups of two to three students will write original lyrics sung to the tune of an easily recognizable song. All groups can write lyrics to the same song or you can allow groups to choose a tune that you approve in advance. Lyrics should follow a simple rhyme scheme and fit the rhythm of the music. Encourage students to create catchy lyrics and hooks that listeners will easily remember. When students are finished, allow them to perform their songs for the class.

DRAW

Draw: Student groups can design mock CD jackets for their songs that feature original artwork, a song title, and their original lyrics. Instruct students to invent a name for their "music group" that will appear on the CD jacket and to use creative fonts, colors, and borders.

ASSESSMENT

✓ Did the student participate in the class discussion?

✓ Did the student contribute to the group?

✓ Did the group create original lyrics for the song?

✓ Did the lyrics match the rhythm and melody of a popular song?

✓ Did the student participate in the performance of the song?

✓ Did the group create a CD jacket that displayed their group name, song title, original lyrics, and artwork?

Storyboards

PREPARE

Prepare: Search online for the word "storyboarding" and visit websites that deal with storyboarding in advertising, animation, or filmmaking. Try to print one or two sample storyboards and bring them to class. In addition, be prepared to provide each student with a poster board or six to eight pieces of plain, white copy paper.

DISCUSS

Discuss: Challenge students to tell the story of *Goldilocks and the Three Bears, The Three Little Pigs*, and any other favorite folk/fairy tales in five sentences or less. Remind students that, since their storytelling is limited, they should focus only on the main events in the story. For instance, the main events for *Goldilocks and the Three Bears* would include the following:

1. The three bears decide to go for a walk while their porridge cools.
2. Goldilocks is lost in the forest. She finds the bears' house and goes inside.
3. She eats the porridge, she breaks a chair, and then she goes upstairs and falls asleep in the baby bear's bed.
4. The bears come home and discover the empty porridge bowls and broken chair. Then, they find Goldilocks in the baby bear's bed.
5. Goldilocks is frightened. She jumps out of the bed and runs all the way home.

Once students have practiced identifying the main points of a story, explain the concept of storyboarding and how it helps authors, animators, and directors visualize the sequence of events that occur in a narrative. Then, pass the sample storyboards you found online around to your students, pointing out that storyboards illustrate only the main events in a story. Can students describe what the storyboard for *Goldilocks and the Three Bears* or *The Three Little Pigs* would look like?

Writing skill: Developing a story arc
In this exercise, students learn how to identify and develop a story arc that traces the beginning, middle, and end of a narrative. Since storyboards highlight the major events that take place in a story, this activity reveals the narrative conventions common to any developed plot. Though fictional texts are the focus here, students can also apply this skill when outlining the main ideas or arguments of non-fiction writing pieces.

Reaching the Reluctant Writer

Storyboards

WRITE

Write: Students will create storyboards for fairy tales, nursery rhymes, favorite films, or historical events that you approve in advance. Remind students to only storyboard texts or events that they have read, viewed, or researched. Students must provide brief, two-to three-sentence descriptions of the major events in the narrative below each illustration. An effective storyboard should demonstrate a student's understanding of the story's arc, or its beginning, middle, and end.

DRAW

Draw: Students will create simple black-and-white or color illustrations depicting the narrative highlights of the story or event they have chosen. Instruct the class to draw their illustrations in boxes above their written descriptions, so that the result looks like a comic book strip. Finally, remind students to make sure each drawing matches the text beneath it.

ASSESSMENT

✓ Did the student participate in the class discussion?

✓ Was the student able to depict the basic plotline within the storyboard panels?

✓ Did the student's storyboard show a clear beginning, middle, and end?

✓ Did the storyboard illustrations act as visual representations of the student's written descriptions?

Survey

PREPARE

Prepare: Collect or save any consumer surveys you encounter on websites, at hotels and restaurants, or that accompany any bills or mail order items you receive. Ad agencies or the marketing departments of your local utility company and bank may also have survey forms. Once you've gathered a variety of surveys, bring them to class for your students to view.

DISCUSS

Discuss: Once they have looked over the surveys, ask students if they can identify the purpose of a survey. As you discuss the survey questions, note that the information requested is in reference to a consumer's opinion. Then, explain that surveys are used to gather information for manufacturers and advertisers, as well as government agencies and political campaigns.

Next, introduce the concept of biased inquiry by writing the question, "Do you think we should stop having math class altogether or just have it one day a week?" on the chalkboard or overhead. Explain that the question is biased because it presents no option for students who enjoy math and would not make a fair survey question. Finally, discuss how biased questions can skew survey results and why language and word choice should be carefully considered when writing survey questions.

Writing skill: Formulating unbiased questions
This exercise challenges students to construct clear, unbiased survey questions that will help them gather information from their peers. Young writers will note the importance of language and word choice in eliciting thorough, insightful responses from readers.

Survey

WRITE

Write: Students will create survey forms designed to gather information about their peers' opinions on a particular issue of interest, such as current bands, cafeteria food, hobbies, aspirations, etc. Survey forms should include a minimum of five questions that are clear and unbiased. Remind students to leave ample space below their questions for their classmates to fill in answers. Once they have completed their survey forms, give students time to gather responses to their questions.

DRAW

Draw: Students can create graphs and charts to represent the data they collect from their survey forms. Instruct students to present their data in a variety of different formats, such as bar graphs, pie charts, line graphs, etc. Also, urge students to label their graphs and use different colors to differentiate student responses.

ASSESSMENT

✓ Did the student participate in the class discussion?

✓ Did the student create survey questions that reflected a personal interest in an issue to which other students could relate and answer?

✓ Were the student's questions clearly worded and unbiased?

✓ Was the student able to graphically represent the data collected?

✓ Did the student create a graph that was easy to comprehend?

Tag Lines

PREPARE

Prepare: Keep a pad and pencil handy when you're watching TV and write down some of the tag lines associated with products or companies, such as "Just do it™" (Nike), "You're in good hands™" (Allstate Insurance), and "It's finger lickin' good™" (Kentucky Fried Chicken). Bring the list of tag lines you compiled to class and share them with your students.

DISCUSS

Discuss: Based on the examples you read aloud, ask students if they can think of any additional tag lines and write them on the chalkboard or overhead. Can students guess why advertisers chose those slogans? Explain that tag lines express the values or nature of a company and that they are created to promote the products and services a company offers. For example, the phrase "Just do it™," which connotes the discipline and fearlessness associated with competitive sports, is the slogan Nike uses to advertise athletic apparel.

Next, ask your students to point out any uses of word play, such as puns, clichés, dialect, or onomatopoeia, in the tag lines discussed. Do students think they are more likely to remember a slogan that features some form of word play? Finally, note that the purpose of a tag line, besides promoting a company's goods and services, is to "stick" in the reader's memory.

Writing skill: Creating a slogan
This activity gives students an opportunity to compose memorable slogans that have popular appeal. In order to write effective tag lines, young writers will have to identify the most important features and benefits of a product or service and create a simple message that strengthens its "brand" image. Students can also experiment with different forms of word play to make their tag lines more humorous or distinctive.

Reaching the Reluctant Writer

Tag Lines

WRITE

Write: Students will write tag lines for your school or classroom. Tag lines should reflect some value or aim of the school or class, such as the subject taught, student and/or teacher goals, student and/or teacher accomplishments, etc. Here are some possible examples:

- Mrs. Weathersby's classroom—"It's the WRITE place"
- Lyon Elementary—"A place to learn, grow, and help others"
- Mr. Richoux's 4th Grade—"We're getting better every day"

Encourage students to use puns, clichés, alliteration, onomatopoeia, and other types of word play to render a more memorable tag line.

DRAW

Draw: Students should design a graphic symbol to accompany their tag line. An image of two hands shaking, an upward-pointing arrow, a hand making a "thumbs up" sign, and a school/class mascot leaping through the air with excitement are all possible examples. Remind students that the graphic does not have to directly correspond to the tag line, but that it should somehow represent the message conveyed.

ASSESSMENT

✓ Did the student participate in the class discussion?

✓ Was the student able to create a tag line for your classroom or school?

✓ Did the tag line convey a positive message or statement that reflected school or class goals and values?

✓ Did the student design an attractive logo to appear with the tag line?

Timelines

PREPARE

Prepare: Search online for various samples of timelines tracing major historical events, stock market averages, or consumer trends over a specific time period. Students need not understand the data represented; the object is simply to show a method of displaying chronological information. Print out and bring any timelines you find online to class, along with a roll of adding machine paper.

DISCUSS

Discuss: Ask students to read over the timelines and identify the different types of information represented. Point out the features common to the timelines, such as specific dates and brief descriptions of major events, and explain that all timelines are essentially historical references. Then, encourage students to name the major historical and cultural events that have taken place during their lifetimes, and write them on the board along with corresponding dates of occurrence.

Next, note that some timelines appear as horizontal or vertical lines representative of a time continuum, while others are detailed through a list of specific dates in bold typeface followed by a paragraph of text describing individual events. Do students prefer one form over the other? Discuss possible reasons for choosing to present chronological information in either format. For instance, do students think it is more practical to display the major events of an entire century on a physical timeline or in a list of significant events? Finally, note the use of any graphics in the sample timelines, and explain that spot art or small images can help readers remember and differentiate the individual dates and/or events featured on a timeline.

Writing skill: Relating events in chronological order
In this exercise, students practice relating events in sequence and presenting information chronologically. Young writers must also choose an accessible format that helps readers retain the information detailed in their timelines. When students are challenged to organize and structure data into a clear, logical layout, they pay attention not only to what but how they are writing.

Reaching the Reluctant Writer

Timelines

WRITE

Write: Students will create timelines tracing at least five significant personal events. Examples could include their birth, moving to a new town, the birth of a sibling, the death of an elderly relative, starting school, a memorable vacation, any personal achievements, etc. Students can display their personal timelines on a horizontal "time continuum" using adding machine paper that you provide, or they can write a list of dates followed by brief descriptions of the major events in their lives. Remind students to choose a format that complements the level of detail featured in their timelines. For instance, students who wish to provide more text about each event should use the list format.

DRAW

Draw: Students should include spot art or small cartoons depicting the events on their timelines. Possible examples include a drawing of a baby to indicate birth or an illustration of a trophy to denote personal achievement.
Also, encourage students to include "background" art that illustrates the passage of time through changes in seasons or the movement from a small town to a big city.

ASSESSMENT

✓ Did the student participate in the class discussion?

✓ Was the student able to identify at least five significant personal events?

✓ Did the student represent the events in chronological order?

✓ Did the student use a timeline format that is clear and accessible?

✓ Did the student include spot art on the timeline?

Troubleshooting Guide

PREPARE

Prepare: Gather owner's manuals from appliances or other items you have purchased, and make copies of the trouble-shooting guides included in each manual. You can also find troubleshooting guides online. Print enough copies to distribute one troubleshooting guide to each student in your class.

DISCUSS

Discuss: Give students a chance read over the trouble-shooting guides and ask them to identify any headings or categories featured, such as "Problem," "Solution," "What happened," "Correction," etc. Also, see if any students have troubleshooting guides that present possible problems in the form of questions (e.g., "Why can't I turn on my computer?") or that take on the voice of the user (e.g., "My computer will not turn on"). Explain that the purpose of writing in this way is to help readers find solutions to their problems as quickly and easily as possible.

Next, talk about how the content in a troubleshooting guide is devised, pointing out that common user problems are often highlighted and presented as "frequently asked questions." Note that the authors of troubleshooting guides must also foresee any difficulties users may have with a product in order to offer effective solutions.

Writing skill: Problem and solution writing
When students write their own troubleshooting guides, they must anticipate user problems and compose clear, comprehensive solutions that will remedy those problems. This exercise challenges students to address their audience and write in a user-friendly manner.

Reaching the Reluctant Writer

Troubleshooting Guide

WRITE

Write: Students will create troubleshooting guides for objects they own and use around their homes or at school. Objects could include bicycles, video game players, small electronics, roller skates, etc. Troubleshooting guides should outline common problems associated with the item and solutions for how to fix them. Remind students to present possible problems in the form of questions or adopt the user's voice to make their guides accessible and user-friendly.

DRAW

Draw: Challenge students to include small graphics in their troubleshooting guides that illustrate how to solve user problems. Drawings should appear alongside problems/solutions and must be labeled and referred to in the text (e.g., "Figure A shows you how to replace the bike chain").

ASSESSMENT

✓ Did the student participate in the class discussion?

✓ Did the troubleshooting guide contain a list of common problems and clear solutions for how to fix them?

✓ Did the student provide accurate solutions to the possible problems identified?

✓ Did the student include graphics to support or clarify text in the troubleshooting guide?

Warning Label

PREPARE

Prepare: Collect warning labels from household products like medicines, food items, cleaning products, tools, or lawn equipment that feature strong or "commanding" verbs. The surgeon general's warnings on cigarette ads are a good example. Bring the labels you gather to class and read them aloud to your students.

DISCUSS

Discuss: Challenge students to write down all the verbs they hear as you read the warning labels. Define the use of strong verbs and text that directly addresses an audience as writing in the "imperative mood." Explain that the imperative mood is commonly used in warning labels to protect consumers from damage to their equipment, personal injury, and even death. Then, note the use of bold colors, large or capitalized typefaces, exclamation points, or graphics in the warning labels you brought to class, and talk about how these visuals also aim to attract a reader's attention.

Writing skill: Writing in the imperative mood
In this exercise, students learn to warn or alert readers by writing in the imperative mood. Young writers will notice that the imperative mood yields an abrupt, terse tone that proves useful when directing readers to take or refrain from taking some action. This activity illustrates how active verbs can strengthen and clarify student writing.

Warning Label

WRITE

Write: Students will create warning labels for something that is potentially dangerous, such as a kitchen knife or an electrical outlet. You can also add humor to the assignment by allowing students to write warning labels for their rooms ("Danger! Dirty room ahead. Watch your step!"), school cafeteria food ("Warning! Monstrous meatloaf. Watch what you eat!"), or younger siblings ("Beware of wild, untamed siblings!"). Students should write in the imperative mood and use "commanding" verbs that will garner attention.

DRAW

Draw: Challenge students to create graphics for their warning labels. Black exclamation points on a yellow background to alert readers, skull and crossbones to indicate toxic chemicals, or flames to denote flammability are just a few examples. Also, encourage students to use fonts and colors that will attract readers.

ASSESSMENT

✓ Did the student participate in the class discussion?

✓ Did the student point out a truly dangerous aspect of the item in the warning label?

✓ Did the student write in the imperative mood by directly addressing the reader and using strong, active verbs?

✓ Did the student design an original graphic image for the warning label?

Websites

PREPARE

Prepare: Schedule time for your class to meet with the school's library media or technology specialist so students can surf the Internet. If you have time beforehand, compile a short list of websites you approve of and ask students to look at those sites specifically.

DISCUSS

Discuss: First, talk about the content featured on each website and how text is organized through the use of headings and links. Do students notice any links common to most websites, such as "Home," "Contact Info," "About Us," etc.? Encourage students to explore any other links available and ask them to point out whether links generally appear at the top, bottom, or along the sides of homepages. Do students find the websites easy to navigate, or is some information hard to find?

Next, challenge your class to identify the websites as informative, promotional, entertaining, or some combination of the three. Then, point out how colors, images, fonts, and general layout vary between these different types of websites. For instance, are flashy graphics and bright colors more likely to appear in promotional websites or do purely informative websites tend to feature less showy, more streamlined layouts? Finally, identify websites as visual texts and explain that layout and appearance are just as important to a website as the content provided.

Writing skill: Designing an accessible layout
In this exercise, students expand their informational writing skills to present text in an accessible format that readers can navigate with ease. The ability to arrange content into a user-friendly layout is an important skill when learning to write everyday texts that rely equally on functional visuals and clear, intelligible writing. This activity challenges students to realize the principles of effective informative writing (e.g., being clear, concise, accessible, and knowing your audience) in a medium that combines images and text.

Websites

WRITE

Write: Students will work in small groups to devise the content for mock websites that promote a product/service, inform, or entertain readers. Websites can promote students' favorite bands, inform readers about sports and sports teams, or entertain users with jokes, poems, or short stories that students write. Groups can also create personal websites that inform readers about individual group members and their hobbies or personal interests.

Websites must include links to the homepage and contact information, as well as three additional links that divide the content provided into different categories. Remind students to write clearly and be specific when creating links and/or headings.

DRAW

Draw: Each group will create an original, color layout for their mock website and draw it to scale on graph paper. Students should draw the web pages that link to their homepage on separate sheets of paper. Encourage them to carefully consider the placement of text and links on their site using the websites they viewed in class as models. Websites must feature graphics, fonts, and colors that relate to and reflect the content written for the site.

ASSESSMENT

✓ Did the student participate in the class discussion?

✓ Did the student contribute to the group?

✓ Did the group write content for an informative, promotional, or entertaining website?

✓ Did the group conceive a layout for their mock website and draw it to scale on graph paper?

✓ Did the group use graphics, fonts, and colors that complement the content created for the website?

A Final Word

Remember that very few of your students will become novelists or playwrights, but every one of them will be an "everyday writer," authoring memos, emails, directions, thank-you notes, and many other less glamorous but essential forms of writing. Therefore, there's no reason why we should pay less attention to the quality of students' "real world" writing than we do to their fiction or poetry. As your students learn and practice writing craft skills, remind them that not all writers pen sonnets or compose literary masterpieces. There are people who make very good livings writing magazine and television advertisements, instruction manuals, and even the backs of cereal boxes.

Finally, encourage your students' parents to let their children see them writing. One of my fondest memories of my father is watching him pay the family bills and sign his name with an incredible flourish. He wasn't just writing a check; he was making a statement. He was writing, he was drawing, and I thought it was wonderful. Likewise, when you allow students to infuse informational texts with humor and artistry you help them discover the strength and uniqueness of their own voices.

I hope this book has been a valuable resource for you and your young writers. Thanks for all you do for the kids.

– Mike Artell

Other Helpful Writing Books

Arnsteen, Katy Keck, Nancy Bentley, and Donna Guthrie. *The Young Author's Do-It-Yourself Book: How to Write, Illustrate, and Produce Your Own Book*. Brookfield, CT: Millbrook Press, 1994.

Artell, Mike. *Write Fast, Write Funny: A Guide to Writing Short Humor*. Grand Rapids: Good Apple, Inc., 1996.

Artell, Mike. *How to Create Picture Books*. Ashland, OH: Monday Morning Books, 1993.

Christelow, Eileen. *What Do Authors Do?* New York: Clarion Books, 1995.

Frank, Marjorie. *If You're Trying to Teach Kids to Write, You've Gotta Have This Book*. Nashville, TN: Incentive Publications, 1979.

Freeman, Marcia S. *Listen to This: Developing an Ear for Expository Writing*. 2nd ed. Gainesville, FL: Maupin House, 1999.

Forney, Melissa. *Razzle Dazzle Writing: Achieving Excellence Through 50 Target Skills*. Gainesville, FL: Maupin House, 2001.

Hoyt, Linda and Margaret Mooney. *Exploring Informational Texts: From Theory to Practice*. Portsmouth, NH: Heinemann, 2003.

Melton, David. *A Revolutionary Two-Brain Approach for Teaching Students to Write and Illustrate Amazing Books*. Kansas City, MO: Landmark Editions, 1985.